Scenes
I've Seen...

**A Casting Director's
Original Scenes
and Interpretive Notes**

A Smith and Kraus Book
Published by Smith and Kraus, Inc.
177 Lyme Road, Hanover, NH 03755
www.SmithKraus.com

First Edition: June 2001
10 9 8 7 6 5 4 3 2 1

Library of Congress Cataloging-in-Publication Data
Scenes I've Seen: a casting director's original scenes
and interpretive notes / by Dorian Dunas.
p. cm. — (Monologue and scene series)
ISBN 1-57525-292-9
1. Scenes. 2. Drama—Collections. 3. Acting. 4. Acting—Auditions.
I. Title. II. Series.
PN2080 .D85 2001
808.82'45—dc21
2001034393

Scenes
I've Seen...

A Casting Director's Original Scenes and Interpretive Notes

by Dorian Dunas

MONOLOGUE AND SCENE SERIES

SMITH AND KRAUS

For Romelle

Acknowledgements

Candy Gonzalez for your much appreciated
encouragement and support.

Ron Dunas for your valued input.

Diane Robin for your contribution to "Joanne and Grace."

Jeff Dunas for your words of advice.

Contents

Introduction vi

MAN and WOMAN • comedy 1

MAN and WOMAN • drama 19

WOMEN • comedy. 35

WOMEN • drama. 53

MEN • comedy. 71

MEN • drama. 89

Introduction

I've been in casting for fourteen years. In that period of time, I've attended countless acting workshops where casting directors bring in scenes for actors to read and then evaluate their performances.

I originally brought in scenes from films I had cast, or I used scenes from films I admired. I constantly searched for new scenes that would have the appropriate format for these workshops. I realized that what I was looking for was difficult to find: scenes that were of a certain length, that involved only two characters, and that allowed the actors to audition with challenging material.

I scoured bookstores, looking for alternative scenes and was rarely satisfied with what I found. Most scenes available are from either recognized plays or movies; the original material found was comprised primarily of shorter scenes than what I was searching for.

Actors often complain about the difficulty in finding new scenes to rehearse. They are looking for material that hasn't already been seen in film or theater and that doesn't leave another actor's performance resonating in their mind. I originally wrote just a few scenes for actors to audition with, but frequently was asked if I had additional material that they could also use for other auditions.

I wrote this book with the hope that actors of all ages would be able to find scenes, both comedic and dramatic, that could be used to further their careers in various types of auditions.

I have included a page of notes to accompany each scene for the purpose of lending additional information and insight about the characters. I believe that the more knowledge an actor has about the role the better qualified they are to make appropriate choices in their performance.

The personal thoughts I offer are from a casting director's point of view. I am not attempting to give advice on acting but rather commenting on what I felt either hindered or enhanced the scenes when I saw them performed.

MAN and WOMAN

❖ ❖ ❖

comedy

Notes to Simon and Ellie Scene

This scene has been one of the favorites of actors, always generating a lot of laughter from the audience.

I have found it most successful when both actors allow their characters to be quirky and amusingly neurotic—really having fun with the scene.

Both Ellie and Simon are compulsive, high-strung, and without question well-suited to each other. Although they argue through most of the scene, the tone should not be mean-spirited and angry. They are not attacking each other but rather pointing out each other's flaws and eccentricities.

The body language in the scene also contributes to the comedy, with Simon pacing and Ellie pacing directly behind him. The more animated he becomes the more he gesticulates, and when she gets unnerved, she begins twirling her hair around her finger.

The scene starts off with Simon almost thinking out loud and eventually snowballs when his anxiety leads him to admit that Ellie might not be the perfect woman for him. He immediately starts backpedaling but only digs himself deeper into a ditch. Ellie retaliates with rightful indignation, and now they're on a roll.

By the end of the scene, both are standing still, feeling awkward and embarrassed by the revelations they've exchanged. They realize more clearly than ever that they are perfectly matched, and their tone becomes one of affectionate teasing.

SIMON AND ELLIE

An engaged couple deal with their impending marriage.
Ellie Randolph and Simon Dunn sit at their dining room table, hav-
ing just finished dinner. Simon fidgets in his chair.

ELLIE: Okay, you've been quiet all night. You want to tell me what's going on?

SIMON: I've been thinking. Maybe we're rushing into this marriage thing…

ELLIE: What? How do you define rushing? We've lived together for three years!

SIMON: Exactly! And they've been very good years, haven't they? So why are we so anxious to change a good thing?
(Ellie pushes her chair back.)

ELLIE: Tell me you're kidding. Tell me you're not having second thoughts four weeks before this wedding!
(Simon rises and begins pacing back and forth in front of the table.)

SIMON: C'mon, you're not? This is forever, Ellie. Nobody in my family has ever gotten divorced. Not even my great uncle, Ivan. And his wife, Sadie, had a mustache and was delusional for thirty years. He didn't divorce her. My cousin, Helen, and her husband threatened each other on a weekly basis with kitchen knives. They didn't get divorced. He finally died of exhaustion. Gave up and let her win…

ELLIE: Simon! What the hell are you going on about? Are you suddenly convinced that we're heading toward divorce? Where did this come from?
(Ellie jumps out of her chair and starts pacing after Simon.)

ELLIE: I wasn't the one that wanted to get married in the first place. You spent six months talking me into this, convincing me we were the perfect couple. Now my mother has bought a dress, sent out the invitations, we've reserved the church, my sister is flying in from Pittsburgh, my brother from California, to say nothing of . . .
(Ellie stops in her tracks.)

ELLIE: Have you met someone else? Is that what this is about?

SIMON: *(Indignant.)* No! Jesus, Ellie, give me some credit. Look, you're an amazing woman. You're virtually everything a man could want. You're 99% of the pie.

ELLIE: 99%?

SIMON: *(Stammering.)* What I mean to say is, you're great. You are…but it's always been a problem for me that you hate baseball.

(Ellie crosses her arms, her eyes narrowing.)

ELLIE: What?

SIMON: Not only do you hate baseball, but I know for a fact, you don't like it when I play my bongos. I like to eat at seven, you prefer eight. What are we supposed to do, spend the rest of our lives compromising at seven-thirty? I, I don't know…

ELLIE: The total tonnage of what you don't know is astounding!

SIMON: Ellie, listen to me. What if we walk down the aisle and I promise to love, honor and cherish till death do us part, and a month later I meet Miss 100%, who not only likes baseball and bongos, but actually prefers me in Hawaiian shirts?

ELLIE: Simon, you are either one of the world's great assholes, which I am just now learning, or your feet are so cold you've got frostbite! You actually think this imaginary woman exists that will love everything about you?

(Ellie begins twirling her hair around her finger, pacing again.)

ELLIE: My God, you hum show tunes under your breath when you read the paper each morning. You bicycle in your sleep! Did you know that? Your legs pump a mile a minute the first hour you fall asleep. Our neighbors are trying to evict us over your bongo playing, and I don't hate baseball! I hate you quoting stats for every pitcher's earn-run-average over the last eight years!

SIMON: See! The truth is finally coming out!

ELLIE: Yes, the truth is you have a lot of annoying habits!

SIMON: *(Facing her.)* And you don't? You roll your hair between your fingers when you get nervous! See?

(Ellie immediately drops her hand to her side.)

SIMON: You love Jerry Lewis movies. Only the goddamn French like Jerry Lewis! You refold the towels in the bathroom every time I get out of the shower so the stripes line up! And best of all, you rearrange the furniture in the apartment every month so I walk around like Helen Keller, knocking over tables!

ELLIE: *(A beat.)* Are you done?

SIMON: Yes. I think so.

(They stare at one another, silent. The corners of Ellie's mouth begin to turn up.)

ELLIE: Do I really line up the stripes?

(Simon nods.)

SIMON: *(Sheepish.)* Do I really bicycle in my sleep?

(Ellie nods.)

SIMON: No one else would put up with us, would they?

ELLIE: That possibility exists.

(Simon hugs her, shaking his head.)

SIMON: I'm sorry, El. It's temporary insanity.

ELLIE: *(Deadpan.)* It's not temporary, Simon. You've always been this way. It's part of your charm...That and the show tunes.

SIMON: It's not too late to call off this wedding!

ELLIE: *(Laughing.)* Shut up, and help me clear the table.

Notes to Louis and Sara Scene

Hopefully, actors will enjoy performing this scene because it allows them to play two different roles; the characters within the play, Louis and Sara, and the actors portraying them, Howard and Julia.

Although the characters are different, ironically the relationship between them is similar. Both Louis and Sara dislike each other, as do Howard and Julia. Yet, Louis is controlled and condescending, while Howard is melodramatic and bitchy. Sara is defensive and biting, while Julia is joyfully snide and dismissive.

The exchange within the office should leave the audience wondering whether the truth lies in Sara's accusations or Howard's indignant denial of them. If that's where the audience's attention is, hopefully they'll be thrown when Louis suddenly stands and talks to the unseen director, revealing that we are witnessing the rehearsal for a play.

At that point, the drama turns to comedy, with the audience enjoying both actors' sense of undeserving self-importance. Neither has been successful in their careers, yet both feel entirely superior to the other.

The scene is enhanced if the actors playing the roles find different body language and rhythm to each character, so there is a distinct separation between them.

LOUIS AND SARA

A nasty confrontation between a man and a woman. Art imitating life. Louis, a well-dressed man in his fifties, sits at his desk, working. There is a knock at the door and Sara, an attractive woman in her thirties, enters.

SARA: You wanted to see me, Louis?

LOUIS: Yes, please come in, Sara, and close the door.

(Sara sits opposite Louis and folds her hands in her lap.)

LOUIS: This is never easy, so I'm going to get right to the point. I've been reviewing your work over the past several months and I'm going to have to let you go.

SARA: *(Stunned.)* I beg your pardon? You're firing me?

LOUIS: I'm afraid I am, yes.

SARA: On what grounds? I've knocked myself out for the past year working for this agency!

LOUIS: Well, that may be your perception, but it doesn't reflect mine.

SARA: I have worked very hard and tried to bring in four new accounts. It isn't for lack of trying, you have to at least give me that!

LOUIS: *(Patronizing.)* Again, it's a difference of opinion. I felt your prospective accounts were sub-standard for this firm. Hardly worthwhile.

SARA: Oh, I see. The sleazy accounts that pay us handsomely are the only ones worth pursuing.

LOUIS: No need to get snide, Miss Parker. It's that very quality of yours that also contributed to your termination, among other...

SARA: Oh, now we're getting to it...

LOUIS: Don't interrupt me when I'm speaking! When my lips are still moving, yours should not be! Do I make myself clear?

(Sara stares at him with venom.)

LOUIS: I haven't been impressed with your creativity on the last three jobs. I think our offer of one week's severance is more than generous.

SARA: *(Jumps up.)* This is crap! I'm the best copywriter here and you know it. You're firing me because I have rebuffed every pathetic attempt you've made to get into my pants!

LOUIS: How dare you! I have made no such attempts and I'm indignant that you would suggest otherwise.

SARA: Is that so? Well, I tell you what, *Louis,* you fire me and I'll file a sexual harassment suit so fast it will make your head spin!

LOUIS: You bitch! You think you can prove it happened?

SARA: You think you can prove it *didn't?*

LOUIS: *(Seething.)* I ought to call security and have you dragged out of here by your ankles.

(Sara smiles smugly and walks around Louis' desk, whispering in his ear.)

SARA: You do that! But keep in mind that as I'm being dragged through the office, I'll be quoting dates and places where you tried to rub up behind me, you repulsive slug!

(Louis abruptly stands and looks beyond Sara, shielding his eyes and squinting off in the distance.)

LOUIS: *(Yelling.)* Okay! This has got to stop! Hugh? Are you listening to me? This is the third day in a row this bitch has eaten garlic at lunch and she knows the smell nauseates me! Hello? Hugh, are you out there? *(No response. Louis turns to Sara.)*

LOUIS: Great. You're so dreadful, Julia, even the director walks out on our rehearsal.

(Sara/Julia also shields the light from her eyes, looking into the darkness, off stage.)

SARA/JULIA: Oh, don't get your panties in a bunch, you old queen. He probably snuck off to the bathroom.

LOUIS/HOWARD: Or maybe he snuck off to your dressing room to wait for your real work to begin.

SARA/JULIA: Are you insinuating I got this job by sleeping with the director?

LOUIS/HOWARD: It's the only explanation I can come up with. God knows it wasn't your abundance of talent, sweetie! If you could learn to act with more than your breasts . . .

SARA/JULIA: Oh, and this is coming from the prince of dinner theatre in Des Moines? Please. Fifteen years of regional theatre performing *Guys and Dolls* hardly qualifies you as Sir Laurence Olivier! I keep forgetting, were you cast as one of the guys or one of the dolls?

LOUIS/HOWARD: That's it. I quit! I've come too far in my career to put up with this shit. You're an unprofessional, untalented, Miss-Runner-Up in a local beauty pageant, stuffed into a pushup bra and you dare to malign *my* career?

(He brushes past her and stomps off stage.)

SARA/JULIA: *(Yelling after him.)* Your career? Hah! At least I was on *Baywatch!* You has-been! You're not even a has-been, you're a never-was!

(She walks offstage, adjusting her cleavage and muttering to herself.)

SARA/JULIA: Pushup bra, my ass! These are all mine, you old twit!

Notes to Norman and Amanda Scene

What is imperative in this scene is the actor's willingness to play Norman with total abandon. He is a blithe spirit, unaware of how truly annoying he is. He sees himself as a smooth operator, insinuating himself into Amanda's company, hoping she'll be impressed with his charm. The fact that he is entirely oblivious to her apparent distaste for him is what gives the scene its comedy.

Amanda starts off the scene trying to be polite to a stranger, but has no idea what she's in for. She is every person who has ever flown on a plane, hoping not to have their flight disrupted by a chatty person seated next to them.

She is initially good-natured, but grows more affronted and finally becomes indignant and mortified by her misfortune. Although Norman is clearly the more comical character, Amanda's responses should participate equally in the humor of the scene.

I saw the scene performed once, where the actor elected to have Norman feign sleep at the end, opening one eye for the audience to see. He explained that he assumed Norman was faking it, hoping to rub up against Amanda. Although it was an interesting choice, I would recommend Norman being genuinely passed out, so the weight of his body and unconscious snoring contribute to Amanda's trapped despair!

NORMAN AND AMANDA

Two strangers meet on a plane.
Amanda Moen sits in an aisle seat, and Norman Crudlip sits directly behind her. After they both settle in, Norman immediately leans over her shoulder and begins talking.

NORMAN: Excuse me, I noticed the seat next to you is empty and I wondered if you wouldn't mind if I joined you? Flying makes me a bit anxious.

AMANDA: *(Turning around.)* Well frankly, I was hoping to spread out a bit and read my book. You know, relax for a few hours.

NORMAN: Of course, I understand.

(Amanda turns back around and adjusts her seat belt. Norman continues, leaning in.)

NORMAN: I wasn't altogether honest. Actually, flying terrifies me. I had to take an Ambien, just to get on the plane.

AMANDA: *(Turning around again.)* You took a sleeping pill for a flight to Phoenix? It's only a two-hour flight.

NORMAN: Yes, but this way it will be a more pleasant two hours! I'm Norman Crudlip, by the way. I don't think I caught your name.

AMANDA: *(Smiles weakly.)* Amanda. Amanda Moen.

NORMAN: Is that right? First girl I ever fell in love with was named Amanda. Cute as a button, she was! Anyway, it's really only the take-off and landing that make me so nervous. I understand most of the accidents happen at those times.

AMANDA: *(Resigning herself.)* Okay. How about if you sit up here just for the take-off then?

NORMAN: Great! I sure appreciate your generosity of spirit.

(He jumps up and moves into the seat next to Amanda, smiling broadly.)

NORMAN: So, what takes you to the lovely town of Phoenix?

AMANDA: My best friend lives there. I'm going for the weekend to visit. How about you?

NORMAN: My aunt, Millie, is getting married. Finally! It hasn't been easy for her. In truth, she's not terribly attractive and has a slight problem with flatulence.

AMANDA: *(Taken aback.)* More information than I needed to have, but thanks for sharing, Norm!

NORMAN: *(Embarrassed.)* Oh, sorry! So, what do you do for a living?

AMANDA: I'm in sales. Ad space for local radio stations. How about you?

NORMAN: I write Hallmark cards.

AMANDA: Really? That must be a fun job.

NORMAN: Oh yes, it's quite fulfilling. Sentiment is a deeply important part of those occasions when you "care enough to send the very best!" When I write, I need to free up the creative juices, so I take off all my clothes and pace back and forth naked with my eyes closed. That generally does the trick.

AMANDA: Norm! Again, more information than I needed!

NORMAN: Right . . . So, I'm guessing you have a boyfriend?

(Amanda gives him a sidelong glance, without responding.)

NORMAN: Oh, come on. Pretty girl like you, there must be someone who lights up your life. If I'm wrong, I'd be delighted, mind you. I'd ask for your number and . . .

AMANDA: Yes! I'm seeing someone! His name is Ron.

NORMAN: Uh-huh. And may I ask how long you've been together?

AMANDA: A year and two months.

NORMAN: Is that right? Has he sent you any Hallmark cards yet?

AMANDA: *(Sardonic.)* Well, no. But there's always hope for the future.

NORMAN: Maybe so, but it seems to me he's already dropped the ball, if you don't mind my saying. I mean, in a year, you've had a birthday, an anniversary, to say nothing of Easter and the winter holidays. Or what about just a lousy day at work, perhaps? Maybe a little card saying, "thinking of you when you're feeling blue!" Now, wouldn't that have lifted your spirits on that particular day?

AMANDA: *(Stifling a smile.)* You clearly are a poetic and insightful man, Norman. Who knew? First impressions can be so deceiving.

(All of a sudden, Norman thinks he feels movement in the plane and shrieks, grabbing Amanda's leg in terror. She shrieks as well.)

NORMAN: Did you feel that turbulence? My heart stopped!

AMANDA: Norman, we're on the ground! Those were the engines starting up the plane!

NORMAN: Well, you screamed too!

AMANDA: I screamed because you grabbed my leg! *(Looking down.)* And your hand is still on my leg, would you remove it please?

NORMAN: Maybe I should leave it there, preparing for real turbulence!

AMANDA: *(Lifting his hand off her leg.)* Not if you want to live through this flight!

NORMAN: Well, excuse me. Here I thought we were becoming good friends.

AMANDA: We are not becoming friends! I don't even know you, nor do I want to! You are the oddest man!

NORMAN: That's a horrible thing to say. I'm deeply offended, Amanda.

AMANDA: Good lord. Look, Norman, I was just trying to be polite when I said it was okay for you to sit here for a few minutes. I wasn't hoping to *bond* with you over the next two hours!

NORMAN: How rude! Frankly, I would think in sales you'd have better interpersonal skills.

AMANDA: Okay, that's it! Move. Go back to your own seat! What is it about me that always attract the weirdos? It's uncanny! I just try to mind my own business and . . .

(Norman's whole body falls against Amanda, and he's out like a light. Her mouth still hanging open, she tries pushing him away, to no avail. He begins snoring loudly on her shoulder. She looks down at him and shakes her head.)

AMANDA: *(Muttering.)* Unbelievable. I'm trapped in Hallmark hell!

Notes to Donald and Eve Scene

This scene centers around the awkwardness of a first date. Never an easy endeavor at any age, perhaps even more difficult when you're nearly sixty and not accustomed to engaging in flirtatious banter with a virtual stranger.

Eve is newly widowed and has spent her entire adult life with one man. This date is the first she has been on since she was twenty years old. She is shy, with a gentle sense of humor and no guile. Her awkwardness and candor lead her to blurt out a question at the end of the date, which is so unexpected that Donald bursts out laughing and, hopefully, so does the audience.

Donald has been widowed for several years and is more comfortable with the dating ritual than Eve. He is sensitive to her discomfort and makes every effort to put her at ease. He's a kind and honorable man and finds himself charmed by Eve's bashfulness and honesty.

The scene is best played with a gentle humor and awkwardness. I imagine Eve's discomfort manifesting itself physically, giving an actress many choices to use with her body language. If the actors choose, the pacing of the scene could also lend itself to awkward pauses or overlapping dialogue, as is commonly heard in conversations with people attempting an initial conversation.

DONALD and EVE

Seated at a restaurant, an awkward first date for a couple in their late-fifties.

EVE: Thank you so much for dinner, Donald. My lamb was delicious, I really enjoyed it.

DONALD: I'm pleased to hear it. You know, Beverly told me you're a fabulous chef yourself, so I thought long and hard about where to bring you for a meal.

EVE: Well, I'm certainly not a *fabulous* chef, but I do love to cook. My husband, Bill, was a fussy eater so I had to come up with all kinds of dishes he'd like. *(Confiding.)* Truth is, he claimed he hated a bunch of things that I secretly added to the recipes for thirty-five years and he never knew the difference!

DONALD: Ah hah! The truth comes out. Under that sweet veneer, you're actually a very sly woman with deep, dark secrets!

EVE: *(Chuckling.)* Oh yes, that's me! Mati Hari in a Kimberly Knits suit.

DONALD: Well, it's a lovely suit and you look lovely in it.

EVE: Thank you. That's nice of you to say. I'm not used to all these compliments.

DONALD: I would have thought your husband told you all the time what a wonderful woman you are.

EVE: Oh, don't get me wrong. Bill was a very loving man. But I suppose that after thirty-five years of marriage, it's easy to take one another for granted.

DONALD: That it is. Men tend to focus on other things and lose sight of what's really precious. All the same, I'm sure Bill considered himself a lucky man having you.

EVE: *(Smiling.)* That's very kind. Beverly said you were a gentleman.

DONALD: She had to lie to convince you to accept a date with me! In fact, I'll bet she's been trying to set you up every night of the week.

EVE: No, not at all. In fact, she told me not to admit this, but you're my first blind date since I lost my husband.

DONALD: Well, I'm honored. *(Teasing.)* Now, what else did she tell you not to admit?

EVE: My age! She recommended shaving ten years off. Problem is, I just know myself, and I can't lie to save my soul.

DONALD: Actually, that information is much more appealing to me than you being ten years younger. Besides, I have a fairly rudimentary knowledge of mathematics and those figures would have made you a genuine child bride!

EVE: See? I never even thought of that. I knew it would've backfired!

DONALD: So. How are we doin' on this first date? Is it as painful as you imagined it would be?

EVE: Hardly! I was afraid I wouldn't even make it through the first hour. I actually tried to remember how to toss my hair, but then I realized I'd end up looking like a *mature* woman with a tic! I'll bet dating doesn't cause you a moment of jitters.

DONALD: Not true. I've been set up with a lot of women since my wife died, but it's still awkward, believe me. Getting the dates is easier though. When you get to be my age, if you're single and still have a regular heartbeat you're considered a real catch!

EVE: *(Smiling.)* Well, I'm not at all surprised that your friends' wives have tried to introduce you to their girlfriends. And my guess is, it has little to do with your healthy ticker.

DONALD: Thank you . . . I think!

EVE: Yes, it was a compliment. You were due for one, yourself.
(Donald reaches for the bill and puts his credit card on the table.)

EVE: You know whenever I use the term *girlfriends,* I think of my grand-daughter who refers to my friends and I as the "girls with the grandma faces!"

DONALD: You never mentioned a granddaughter. How old is she?

EVE: She's five and so cute! Her name is Laney.

DONALD: Do you have a picture with you?

EVE: *(Giggles.)* No. I was afraid if I brought one, I'd be tempted to drag it out during the salad course. You get me started on Laney and I can talk all night!

DONALD: Well, maybe when I take you home, you'll invite me in so I can see some pictures of her.
(Eve suddenly freezes and looks at Donald, like a deer caught in head-lights.)

EVE: You weren't planning on getting *lucky* tonight, were you?

DONALD: *(Erupts in laughter.)* Getting lucky? Ah, no. No, I certainly wasn't!

EVE: *(Mortified.)* Oh, what an awful question! Please forgive me. I can't believe I said that . . . I wasn't sure how men made passes these days and I knew I'd be panicked on the way home unless I cleared the air now.

DONALD: Well, I'm glad we got that out of the way, then!

(Eve stands up and covers her face in embarrassment.)

EVE: I'm going to the ladies room. Hopefully I'll have the courage to come back.

DONALD: I'll take care of the bill and we'll get going. And by the way, Eve, I'm not that smooth, so hopefully I'll have the opportunity to make a real pass someday, but I'll give you fair warning. I promise!

(Donald signals for the waiter as Eve shakes her head, smiling sheepishly. She walks off.)

MAN and WOMAN

❖ ❖ ❖

drama

Notes to David and Laura Scene

This couple has been married for five years, and the marriage has slowly disintegrated due to David's drinking.

Laura is the child of an alcoholic and is reliving her childhood drama with David. She has stayed with him out of love and the unrealistic expectation that he will give up drinking. When she discovers she is pregnant, the knowledge that their child will be exposed to the tumultuous upbringing she endured forces her to take action and leave her husband.

David is a man who started as a social drinker in his twenties and progressively has grown more dependent on alcohol to get through each day. He lives in denial about the extent of his problem and how his actions have effected both his life and Laura's. He can usually charm his way back into his wife's good graces, but not on this night.

I saw this scene performed beautifully by actors who understood the quiet drama and tragedy in the lives of these characters. This is not a raging drunk and his angry wife but rather a desperate man and a sadly resigned woman.

Laura's emotions range from anger and hurt to compassion and pity. Her resolve has enabled her to emotionally withdraw from David, finally giving her the strength to leave him.

David walks in, unaware of the many facts that have led up to Laura's decision. He is initially apologetic, then defensive. When confronted with all he stands to lose, he is left in a state of panic and despair, all the more frightening to face without the aid of alcohol.

DAVID and LAURA

A woman confronts her alcoholic husband with news that will change their lives.

Laura sits alone on the couch, her purse and coat by her side, her head in her hands. The door opens and her husband David enters, drunk, and weaving slightly. She looks at him without a word and shakes her head.

DAVID: What? Bud and I watched the game at Hooligans and it went into overtime.

LAURA: Do you know what day it is today?

DAVID: Yeah, it's Monday. So what?

LAURA: It's Monday, the fourteenth. Of November. Our anniversary.

DAVID: *(Winces.)* Oh, shit. Laura, I'm sorry. Look, it's not too late, I'll take you to dinner. C'mon, we'll go somewhere nice.

LAURA: I ate already.

DAVID: Then I'll take you tomorrow night, how's that? Anywhere you want.

LAURA: *(Matter-of-fact.)* I'm leaving you, David.

DAVID: Oh, for Christ's sakes! I fucked up. I said I'm sorry. I didn't do it on purpose. It slipped my mind.

LAURA: Everything slips your mind. That's what happens to drunks. They get forgetful.

DAVID: I am not a drunk, Laura! I have a few drinks with dinner . . .

LAURA: *(Jumps up.)* You have more than a few drinks and you start in the afternoon, not at dinner! There isn't a day that goes by that you're not tanked by eight o'clock!

DAVID: That's crap!

LAURA: It's the truth! You won't even admit you *have* a problem. I've lived with it for five years and I can't do it anymore! I can't.

DAVID: Would you stop with the melodrama! I do not have a drinking problem and you are not leaving me. I've had a lot on my mind and I forgot about our anniversary, I'm sorry!

LAURA: Right, I'm sure losing your job can give you a lot to think about. *(David looks away, and sits down without a word.)*

LAURA: Were you planning on telling me about it or did that slip your mind too?

DAVID: How'd you know?

LAURA: I called the office and they said you no longer worked there. Imagine my surprise.

DAVID: It just happened a few days ago. I was gonna tell you . . .

LAURA: This is the second job you've lost in a year! Your drinking is out of control and it's the reason you keep getting fired!

DAVID: It's not the reason! These companies keep cutting back and the new guy is always the first to get laid off.

LAURA: *(Sadly.)* Dave, you need help. You live your life in denial and I can't keep begging you to get into a program.

DAVID: I'm not having this conversation again. I'm tired, and I'm going to sleep.

(He stands up and turns to leave the room.)

LAURA: David, I'm pregnant.

DAVID: *(Stunned.)* What?

LAURA: That's why I'm leaving.

DAVID: What are you talking about?

LAURA: I'm not raising a child with an alcoholic. I won't subject my kid to what I went through.

DAVID: Laura, I am not your father! I am not erratic and violent!

LAURA: I don't care! You're a drunk, nonetheless. I'm moving in with my sister. If you want to raise this child together, you start going to AA meetings everyday.

(David's eyes well up.)

DAVID: Laura, don't leave me.

LAURA: I'm due in June. If you can show me chips for seven months of sobriety, I'll come back.

DAVID: *(Barely audible.)* Don't do this. Please stay.

(Laura walks over to him and puts her hand on his cheek.)

LAURA: I can't . . . I love you with all my heart, but I can't.

(David's hands start shaking and he stands up and starts to walk across the room.)

LAURA: Don't bother looking. I threw all the bottles out.

(He spins around and they stare at each other, his eyes filled with panic, hers with sadness. She picks up her purse and coat and walks out the door.)

Notes to Ben and Elizabeth Scene

This scene has as much to do with what is unspoken as what is said. The relationship between Elizabeth and her father is formal and ill at ease. They have never shared a warm and intimate relationship, but since the death of Elizabeth's mother, the strain between them has worsened.

Elizabeth was very close to her mother, Lorraine, a warm and loving woman. She was the glue that held the family together and compensated for her husband's stoic demeanor. She was the one Elizabeth could talk to, confide in, and her death left an enormous hole in her daughter's life.

Ben is a man who keeps his emotions locked up, never one to allow his vulnerability to show. He is a wealthy, refined man, concerned with social etiquette and his stature in society. Ben loves his daughter, but is incapable of showing her the warmth and intimacy that she desperately needs from him.

Elizabeth's emotions are very close to the surface. She has a hard time masking the sadness and resentment she feels toward her father. The announcement of his impending marriage triggers a wealth of emotions in Elizabeth, culminating in an honest outburst, its truth causing Ben enormous discomfort.

BEN and ELIZABETH

An estranged father and daughter discuss his recent engagement.
Ben, an elegant man in his sixties, and his thirty-year-old daughter,
Elizabeth, sit at an upscale restaurant in Boston, having lunch. The ten-
sion between them is palpable.

BEN: So? How is everything at the firm? Bill Meredith is treating you well,
I trust?

ELIZABETH: I'm doing the usual grunt work they expect of first year asso-
ciates, Father. Bill Meredith isn't showing me any special treatment
because he's a friend of yours, but I'm sure you didn't expect he would.

BEN: No, I expect he hired you because he knew you'd be an asset to the
firm, and you will be. You graduated first in your class and you're
going to be an outstanding lawyer. I never had any doubt about it.

ELIZABETH: *(Offhand.)* Well, coming from you, that's a real boon.

BEN: Elizabeth, I'm very proud of your accomplishments and I would think
you know that. Why can't you offer a simple "thank you," and leave
it at that?

ELIZABETH: *(A beat.)* You're right, I apologize. Thank you for the vote of
confidence.

BEN: Are you still seeing that architect fellow, Richard Morgan?

ELIZABETH: No, we stopped seeing each other a few months ago. Father,
what's on your mind? I can't imagine that you asked me to lunch to
discuss my social life.

(Ben pauses uncomfortably, then clears his throat.)

BEN: No, I wanted to tell you that Barbara and I are getting married. We're
planning a party in two weeks to announce the engagement and I
would like you to be there.

ELIZABETH: *(Stunned.)* My mother has been dead less than a year and you're
already getting married again? Apparently it didn't take you too long
to get over the grief, did it? You disgrace her memory!

BEN: Elizabeth, keep your voice down, we're in public! I am in no way
disgracing your mother's memory. I loved Lorraine and miss her to
this day, but my life has to go on and I'm lucky to have found a lovely
woman to spend the remainder of my life with.

ELIZABETH: Oh, she's lovely, is she? She's a gold digger who wasted no time circling around you like a vulture in the Mojave dessert. Mom wasn't dead two months before that woman started inviting you over for dinner. She played you like a fiddle!

BEN: How dare you speak to me that way? I won't have it . . .

ELIZABETH: What did you expect? Did you actually think I was going to be happy about this? Apparently you can replace a wife, but I can't replace a mother! Do you understand that?

BEN: I'm not replacing anyone, Elizabeth! You're reacting like a child. I don't expect Barbara to take the place of your mother, or for you to love her in the same way, but I do expect that you will offer her the respect and warmth that I feel she deserves.

ELIZABETH: I don't really give a damn what you expect!

(Elizabeth takes a moment, trying to collect herself before continuing.)

ELIZABETH: Have you told William?

BEN: Yes, I phoned him this morning. He offered his congratulations. Apparently, he's able to accept this more graciously than you are.

ELIZABETH: Of course. Always the good son. William wouldn't know how to express an honest emotion if it hit him over the head.

BEN: Elizabeth, William and I both experienced great loss, but obviously we have the capacity to mourn your mother and yet still carry on. Why do you resent us for that?

ELIZABETH: Is that really what you believe? I carried on myself, for Christ's sake. I buried my mother, finished law school and moved back to Boston without missing a beat. I don't resent anyone's ability to carry on, it's what's expected in this family! What I resent is that not once have I been able to have a conversation with you or my brother about how much I miss my mother! Why can't either of you let me talk about her? I'm not like you two. I can't bury everything in some deep dark place and never confront it. I can't!

(Tears stream down Elizabeth's face, her outburst clearly making her father uncomfortable. He offers her his handkerchief, then glances around the restaurant and speaks quietly.)

BEN: Lizzy, I had no idea this was still so difficult for you. I should have. I know how close you and Lorraine were.

(Elizabeth dries her eyes and lays the handkerchief back on the table.)

ELIZABETH: Whose idea was it to get married so soon? Yours or Barbara's?

BEN: It was both of ours.

ELIZABETH: I see. *(Looks at her watch.)* I hope you don't mind, but I'm not very hungry anymore and I should get back to the office.

(Ben reaches across the table and puts his hand on Elizabeth's wrist.)

BEN: Elizabeth, please. Obviously, this isn't easy for you to accept, but I would appreciate you attending the party and extending yourself accordingly.

ELIZABETH: *(Pained.)* Naturally, father. I wouldn't dream of being honest in front of your guests. I can't even be honest with you.

(Elizabeth gathers her coat and purse and walks out of restaurant, leaving her father alone at the table.)

Notes to Jamie and Alan Scene

Friendships between men and women are difficult to maintain when one person has feelings that aren't reciprocated by the other. This scene reflects that scenario, with Alan harboring romantic and sexual desires that Jamie wants to deflect.

The two have been friends for years, but Jamie knows that Alan isn't remotely her type. She adores him in a fraternal way and wants to keep the relationship purely platonic. She has tried to make that clear to Alan but has never addressed it bluntly, fearing that the truth would hurt him and damage their friendship.

Having misread her affection, Alan believes that he and Jamie are destined to become lovers. Although he has humorously pursued her in the past, this night he's determined to find out what Jamie's reservations are about taking it to the next step.

This scene is both dramatic and comedic. It begins with a light tone, which turns into honest and revealing admissions from both characters. Alan attempts to conceal his damaged ego with glibness and self-deprecating humor, but Jamie knows he's hurt and plays along, trying to ease their mutual discomfort.

JAMIE and ALAN

A man and woman explore the truth about taking their friendship to another level.
Jamie and Alan enter Jamie's apartment late at night, laughing.

JAMIE: That movie was painful. I can't believe you made me sit through the whole thing. Two hours of my life I'll never get back.

ALAN: Quit whining! I made up for it. I paid for dinner.

JAMIE: Oh, yeah, a chilidog and fries. You're a big sport!

ALAN: It's the thought that counts.

JAMIE: *(Yawning.)* I know. I'm just giving you grief. Listen, I got up early and I'm exhausted. I'm going to bed.

ALAN: You want some company?

JAMIE: Don't start in with that again!

ALAN: I'm not starting in with anything. I'm asking a perfectly legitimate question.

JAMIE: Al, we're friends. Friends don't sleep together.

ALAN: What is that? A hard and fast rule? Who better to sleep with than a friend? At least you're guaranteed you'll laugh together if the sex is a disaster!

JAMIE: You're absolutely undaunted, aren't you? It doesn't matter how many times I say no. You still ask why.

ALAN: Exactly. And if you were able to give me a reason that made sense, I'd quit asking.

JAMIE: No you wouldn't.

(Alan walks over to Jamie and puts his hands on her shoulders.)

ALAN: Jamie, answer me this. Are you attracted to me or not? Simple question.

JAMIE: Yes, but . . .

ALAN: But what?

JAMIE: But I'm not interested in starting a relationship.

ALAN: Well, why not? Attraction is a good place to start.

JAMIE: Alan, why are you willing to jeopardize a good friendship?

ALAN: *(Annoyed.)* Because I think it could lead to something better than just friendship! How do you know what you could feel unless you're willing to try?

JAMIE: *(Uncomfortable.)* Because I know what I don't feel.

(Taken aback, Alan looks at her for a moment, without speaking.)

JAMIE: I'm sorry. You asked for the truth, so there it is.

ALAN: I've gotta tell you, I'm confused. We have a great time together. We laugh, we talk. What is it that's missing here?

JAMIE: Just leave it alone, would you? No matter what I say, it's gonna hurt you and I don't want to do that.

ALAN: *(Angry.)* No, I'd really like an answer. Since I've known you, you've gone through three guys, all of whom were assholes. What was it about *them* exactly that jump-started your heart?

JAMIE: *(Defensive.)* I don't know, maybe an element of danger, okay? I admit it! I like guys that are elusive and a little wild. It's probably not the healthiest thing, but it's what works for me!

ALAN: So there's no challenge with me, is that what you're saying? I'm not wild enough for you?

JAMIE: Al, I love you dearly. You're like a brother to me. You're one of the world's nicest guys . . .

ALAN: There it is, the kiss of death! Whenever a woman starts in with, "you're a nice guy," you might as well kill yourself.

JAMIE: Stop it! Being nice is a good thing. Most women spend their lives wanting to meet a guy like you.

ALAN: No they don't. They just say they do. In truth, they're all like you. Running after pricks that are gonna break their heart.

(Jamie pauses for a moment, then responds with a wry smile.)

JAMIE: That's why so many of us are in therapy.

ALAN: This is very depressing.

JAMIE: No it isn't. It's good. We finally cleared the air.

ALAN: I liked it better before, when I thought I still had a shot.

JAMIE: *(A beat.)* Is this gonna ruin our friendship?

ALAN: *(Offhand.)* No. Truth is, it will be easier. Now that I know I'll never end up in your pants, I can give up deodorant and mouthwash.

(She affectionately smacks his arm and walks him to the door.)

JAMIE: Go home, honey. I'll see you soon.

ALAN: Maybe. Maybe not. I'm considering becoming elusive and undependable.

(Alan cracks a smile and closes the door behind him.)

Notes to Matthew and Anne Scene

This is a couple whose animosity destroyed their marriage and now threatens to scar their child. Recently divorced, and still hostile toward one another, they come together to acknowledge the damage they have imposed on their son and the need to rectify the situation.

Matthew is a man whose childhood was filled with the rage of his own parents, and he has carried that distrust and anger through his life. He has a hard time taking responsibility for his behavior until confronted by the reality that his son is repeating his childhood emotions and most likely will become an unhappy adult like he is.

Anne admits participating in their acrimonious marriage, but is far more sensitive to her son's distress and is willing to accept blame for her responsibility. She is filled with self-recrimination and sorrow and is willing to take the necessary steps to create harmony with her ex-husband.

The choice in how this scene is performed entirely effects the outcome. I have seen it several times and the differences were remarkable. If the scene is played with melodrama, it loses all the complexity of the character's varied emotions and can sound like a bad soap opera. If played with honesty and subtlety, the reaction is powerful.

The scene opens with Anne determined to have a civil conversation with her ex-husband. Matthew immediately becomes defensive and biting. Like a knee-jerk reaction, they launch into their familiar accusations and anger. The whole tone of the scene shifts when Anne admits that their anger is toxic and their relationship must change.

For the remainder of the scene, she talks to Matthew not with anger but with sadness. The honesty she expresses leads him to respond in kind, finally acknowledging the impact their bitterness has had on their son.

MATTHEW and ANNE

Divorced parents discuss their troubled child.
Anne sits alone in a chair, staring off in space. She hears a knock on the
door and hesitates a moment before opening it. Matthew enters and the
two stand, uneasily regarding one another.

MATTHEW: What's going on, Anne? Why couldn't we handle whatever this
is over the phone?

ANNE: Can you sit down please? This is important, Matthew.

MATTHEW: *(He remains standing.)* What? Your alimony check was late?

ANNE: *(Measured.)* No. This is not about money. This is not about our
divorce. This is about our son.

MATTHEW: What happened? Is he all right?

ANNE: He got into another fight at school today. He punched Billy Steiger
in the eye.

MATTHEW: Well, that Steiger kid is a pain in the ass. He probably deserved
it.

ANNE: Billy is his best friend. His only friend.

MATTHEW: What are you talking about, his only friend? Jesse has a lot of
friends.

ANNE: Is that what he tells you? Matthew, nobody wants to play with him
anymore, or have him at their birthday parties.

MATTHEW: Well, what the hell is that all about? Jesse's a great kid!

ANNE: Yes, he is a great kid. But since the divorce, he's angry all the time
and doesn't know what to do with it. I don't know what to do with it.

MATTHEW: He's not angry when he's around me. What are *you* doing to
him?

ANNE: *(Hissing.)* Stop it! Stop blaming me! You did that for nine years
and never once took responsibility for your contribution to our prob-
lems. I am not to blame for our marriage falling apart. *We* are to blame.
Both of us!

MATTHEW: You gave up, Anne! You walked out and took my son!

ANNE: You're damn right I did. I didn't think it was healthy for Jesse to
be around two people who did nothing but scream at each other. Is
that what you wanted for him?

MATTHEW: *(Biting.)* It isn't what I wanted for myself.

ANNE: Well, unlike you, I care more for my child, than I do myself.

MATTHEW: Oh Christ, aren't you self-righteous!

ANNE: Fuck you, Matthew!

> *(The two stand, glaring at each other across the room. Anne takes a deep breath and sits down on the couch.)*

ANNE: This has gotta stop. This anger is toxic and it's poisoning our son.
> *(A beat.)*
>
> I've taken Jesse to see a therapist.

MATTHEW: Without consulting me?

> *(Anne's eyes fill with tears.)*

ANNE: He starts fights all the time. He argues with his teacher every day.

MATTHEW: When did this start? Why didn't you tell me about . . .

ANNE: *(Interrupting.)* He's made up an imaginary friend named Sam that he talks to all the time. He insists I set an extra place at the dinner table for him.

MATTHEW: And what does this therapist say about it, that he's nuts?

ANNE: No, that he's lonely! His world doesn't feel safe anymore. He's a seven-year-old little boy who's sad and confused and angry. Apparently, Sam is a companion who comforts him.

MATTHEW: I don't understand. We're both there for him. We love him desperately, he knows that.

ANNE: Not enough, obviously. Dr. Sherman wants us all to come in together to see him.

MATTHEW: Fine.

ANNE: He is the best thing we did, Matthew. He's an amazing child. But our anger at each other ate us up, and no matter how hard we tried to keep it from him, obviously we failed.

MATTHEW: Anne, divorce is hard on kids, I know that. But it's hardest in the beginning and then it works itself out. It doesn't have to mean that Jesse is permanently scarred.

ANNE: Are you kidding? I saw what your parents' divorce did to you. They couldn't even be civil to one another. You don't think their venom is largely responsible for your hostility?

MATTHEW: Oh, give me a fucking break.

ANNE: Matthew, can't you at least admit that much? We are responsible for what our child is going to grow up to be! You learn through example and we have *failed* at setting a good example. If this doesn't stop, the damage will be irreparable!

MATTHEW: *(Winces.)* Set up the time with the shrink. I'll be there . . . We'll work it out, Anne.

ANNE: We'd better.

(He nods and walks out the door, closing it quietly behind him.)

WOMEN

❖ ❖ ❖

comedy

Notes to Joanne and Grace Scene

Joanne and Grace have been best friends for fifteen years. Their personalities are as different as night and day. Joanne is a dreamer, an optimist, and an eternal romantic. Grace is pragmatic, skeptical and glib. Joanne is high-strung and animated, while Grace is dry and deadpan.

Throughout their friendship they've probably had a hundred conversations revolving around the polarity between their approaches to life; Joanne is a flyer, willing to go out on a limb and lead with her heart rather than her head. She is undaunted in her belief that love and passion overcome all obstacles. Grace is practical and weary and rarely finds herself in emotional chaos.

Grace worries that Joanne will spend a lifetime being involved in love affairs that are chaotic and unreliable, while Joanne fears that Grace's pragmatism will prevent her from ever abandoning herself to the possibility of passion and romance.

The pacing of the scene is important, with comedic bantering back and forth, until midway through the scene, where Grace tells Joanne that she's not judging her, but is truly concerned about her getting hurt. The actresses need to allow the tone to shift to a more serious exchange about how they each choose to lead their lives, before it reverts back to the humorous repartee that finishes the scene.

The scene benefits enormously if the actresses can create a believable ease between them, so they can mock each other with the familiarity and fondness that a close friendship allows.

Whenever this scene has been performed, it always illicits great laughter from the audience, particularly from women, who can recall similar conversations they've had with friends of their own.

JOANNE and GRACE

Two old friends sit in Joanne's apartment, discussing her affair with a married man.
Joanne is furiously pacing back and forth, while Grace sits nearby at a table, eating a piece of cake.

JOANNE: That short, fat fuck! That Guinea bastard! I can't believe he's standing me up on my birthday!

GRACE: More cake?

JOANNE: Oh, yeah, fatten me up, so I become even more pathetic and no one will want me.

GRACE: *(Deadpan.)* No one wants you now.

JOANNE: *(Stops pacing and turns to Grace.)* Remind me again why I call you my friend?

GRACE: Because I baked you a Betty Crocker birthday cake and I'll clean up the rug after you slit your wrists.

JOANNE: He promised he'd take me to Spago tonight.

GRACE: Well, I guess his wife's projectile vomiting put a dent in those plans.

JOANNE: I know she got the goddamn flu just to spite me!

GRACE: Jo, she doesn't even *know* about you.

JOANNE: Psychic bitch.

(Grace stifles a laugh.)

JOANNE: Oh, Gracie, why? Why can't he leave her and marry me?

GRACE: Honey, we've had this conversation fifty times. Nothing has changed. He is never going to marry you. Do you honestly believe he will?

JOANNE: Why not? I love him. He loves me.

GRACE: I love my cat. He loves me. I don't think Whiskers is going to marry me!

JOANNE: *(Glaring.)* He promised me he'd leave her as soon as her hives clear up.

GRACE: Her hives? Joanne, don't you see a pattern here? Last month, it was bunions! And the month before, she had some chronic nasal drip. Christ Almighty, this man must consult a medical dictionary for excuses!

JOANNE: Stop it! You don't know Tony. You've never even met him.

GRACE: Well, other than the day I stopped by unexpectedly and passed him skulking by in the hallway. I guess that wasn't a real introduction, though.

JOANNE: He wasn't skulking!

GRACE: How would you know? You were inside the apartment, basking in the afterglow of illicit sex.

JOANNE: He *is* fabulous in bed!

GRACE: *(Snide.)* Well then, forget what I said. He's a real keeper.

JOANNE: Grace, he makes me very happy most of the time. Stop giving me grief.

GRACE: He does not make you happy! Are you on drugs or experiencing short-term memory loss? You do nothing but cry about this man.

JOANNE: It's complicated. Okay? If you weren't so judgmental, you'd understand that.

GRACE: I am not judgmental! Jo, this is not a morality issue. This isn't about the sins of adultery. This is about you suffering because you've loved a married man for a year, and he's promised the moon and the stars, and all he's delivered is a bunch of earth-shaking nooners!

JOANNE: Well, who do you know who hasn't suffered? What couple has a perfect relationship? You think I should walk away now, because it may not work out. But maybe it will! There are no guarantees, Grace. You should know that. Shit, you spent two years thinking Alan was a prince, and he turned out to be the putz of the western world!

GRACE: *(A beat.)* Thank you for that reminder.

JOANNE: Look, if you're going to start throwing stones . . .

GRACE: I wasn't throwing stones! I'm not trying to hurt you. I'm concerned. I'm worried.

JOANNE: *(Softly.)* I know. And I appreciate it. But you and I are different. You live a safe life. I don't. What should I be doing? Dating men I'm not interested in just because they're single? Be alone all the time? I'd rather have some happiness, than none at all.

GRACE: All right. Just don't sell yourself short. You're entitled to more than just *some* happiness.

JOANNE: You know what? When I know he's coming over, I get so excited

I dance around in my underwear. Singing! Now when was the last time some guy made you that happy?

GRACE: *(Chuckling.)* Please. I wouldn't even submit my cat to that visual.

JOANNE: Well, he *is* going to leave his wife.

GRACE: Uh-huh.

JOANNE: He is! They don't even sleep in the same room anymore.

GRACE: And you know this, how?

JOANNE: I sat outside his house the other night and I saw the lights go off in two different rooms.

GRACE: *(Jumps up.)* Oh my God! You're parked outside your lover's house in the middle of the night, spying? This is terrifying.

JOANNE: *(Gleefully.)* No it isn't. I felt very optimistic driving home! C'mon, how long can any couple last sleeping in separate rooms?

GRACE: My parents are still married. They haven't slept in the same room since the sixties!

JOANNE: *(Walking to the door and opening it.)* You can leave now.

GRACE: *(Smiling.)* I'm going, I'm going.

(Grace walks to the door and kisses Joanne on the cheek.)

GRACE: Finish the cake. Italian men like their women plump!

Notes to Holly and Mia Scene

Unlike the other scenes where the difference in characters defines the relationship, this scene relies on the similarities in Holly and Mia. These are two sisters who share a very similar sense of humor and outlook on life. Although Mia is the elder sister and more settled in her life than Holly, they are kindred spirits in relation to the rest of their family.

In most family gatherings, there are predictable interactions that occur, and each person plays a role in that dynamic. As these sisters discuss that subject, they do it with humor, self-deprecation, and ultimately, an honest moment of sadness.

This scene relies on the familiarity between the sisters; a lifelong camaraderie they share. Like any two people with a shared history, they can finish each other's sentences, appreciate the same references, and yet each plays a distinctive role in relation to the other.

Mia is the organizer, the elder sister who has taken on the maternal role of hosting family events. She is more controlling and likes to keep things on an even keel. Holly is the youngest and enjoys her role as the renegade. She likes stirring up trouble, if for no other reason than to agitate Mia. They know how to push each other's buttons, but their sarcasm comes from the safe place of intimacy and affection.

HOLLY and MIA

Holly and her older sister, Mia, discuss their upcoming family holiday.

HOLLY: . . . Just as we're nearing the climactic moment, he screams out, "Tell me I'm your king!"

MIA: You're lying!

HOLLY: Swear to God. I laughed so hard I fell off the bed!

MIA: I would have collapsed!

HOLLY: Needless to say, I won't be seeing him again.

MIA: Where do you find these lunatics?

HOLLY: They find me! Obviously, I've got some defective gene that attracts 'em.

MIA: You know, I dropped you on your head when you were a baby. That probably explains a lot.

HOLLY: Funny.

MIA: Listen, as amusing as your sex life is, can we change the subject and deal with Thanksgiving? What are you gonna bring?

HOLLY: As long as I can buy it and not cook it, I'll bring anything you need.

MIA: Lazy cow.

HOLLY: I am not a lazy cow, I'm a lousy cook! How 'bout if I bring the wine?

MIA: Fine, but come early and help me set the table at least.

HOLLY: Okay. How many have we got this year? Assorted in-laws, or just our dysfunctional family?

MIA: Happily, it's just the seven of us. John and me, Lee and Inger, Dad, Carmella, and you. That is unless you want to invite the king? I could put a little crown next to his plate!

HOLLY: Cute. I should bring him, maybe he'd disrobe at the table and make a pass at Inger. That would keep things lively!

MIA: Oh yeah, the ice queen getting flashed, that would be fun.

HOLLY: I swear, under that cool veneer, she's a tramp waiting to happen. I know she's cheating on Lee.

MIA: What are you talking about?

HOLLY: I saw her coming out of Orso's Tuesday afternoon with her arms around a real swarthy looking guy. Definitely not our brother.

MIA: Maybe it was an old friend or something.

HOLLY: Please, the woman has no friends! How do I tell Lee?

MIA: You don't! Are you out of your mind? There's probably nothing to it, and all you'll do is start trouble.

HOLLY: Where is your loyalty? Wouldn't you want me to tell you if I saw John with some woman?

MIA: No! I know John wouldn't cheat on me, so I'd just assume you were making something out of nothing, and it would piss me off.

HOLLY: Jesus, shoot the messenger! I'd sure want to know if my husband was cheating on me.

MIA: Well, if you ever get married, I'll keep that in mind. In the meanwhile, do not upset Lee and screw up this holiday.

HOLLY: Fine! . . . Is Carmella bringing her infamous avocado and green Jell-O this year?

MIA: *(Nodding.)* She insisted. We're doomed! Someone must have given her that recipe as a joke and the American humor escaped her.

HOLLY: What is it Dad sees in her? It's gotta be the tight sweaters and pointy bras.

MIA: I'm afraid she's gonna give him a heart attack.

HOLLY: *(Shaking her head.)* I know. I stopped by one day and Dad answered the door, all flustered. Carmella was standing behind him in her peek-aboo nightie. It was one in the afternoon, for Christ's sake!

MIA: Well, Dad's married to an over-the-hill sex kitten and Lee's got himself a frozen Nordic princess. I married a man who tells horrible jokes and belches in public, and the men you end up with defy description!

HOLLY: Poor Mom. She must see all of us and roll over in her grave.

MIA: She was the only normal one in the bunch . . . Okay, here's what we have to look forward to; Lee and Inger will snipe at each other. Dad will eat too much and grope Carmella . . .

HOLLY: . . . I'll drink too much wine and get nauseous. John will regale us with dirty limericks and you'll whine that everyone was late and ruined your dinner. Another fun-filled holiday!

MIA: Well, look at it this way; at least we're colorful.

HOLLY: Yeah, right!

(She hesitates a moment, then asks Mia, seriously.)

HOLLY: You think anyone has a normal family and actually enjoys Thanksgiving?

MIA: If they're out there, I haven't met 'em.

HOLLY: That's what I thought.

(They exchange a rueful shrug, and then smile.)

Notes to Nell and Rosie Scene

Nell and Rosie are two waitresses working a busy night at an upscale Italian restaurant.

Throughout the scene, they not only talk to each other, but also talk to an offstage chef, Arturo.

Nell is a high-spirited girl in her twenties, animated and easily amused. She's not a proficient waitress, nor does she aspire to be. She's constantly late to work, tells the customers what they should order, and then eavesdrops on their conversations. Rosie is convinced that if Nell didn't have such a cute face and perky figure, Arturo would have canned her months ago.

Rosie is an easy-going, middle-aged, stocky woman, who has been waiting tables for twenty years. She's married with kids, and her maternal nature extends to everyone that works at the restaurant, except Arturo, whom she refuses to take lip from.

In this exchange, it's important for the actresses to generate different energy. Nell's excitable nature is in counterpoint to Rosie's laid-back demeanor. Physically, they should be standing side by side, talking, but at the same time, keeping their eyes on their respective tables, and looking over their shoulders to direct their remarks to Arturo.

NELL and ROSIE

Two waitresses hover near the kitchen, passing time between orders.
Rosie, a good natured, middle-aged woman leans against the wall, wait-
ing on an order as Nell, a high-strung girl in her twenties, approaches
and yells out to the chef in the kitchen.

NELL: Arturo! I'm still waiting on those eggplant lasagnas for table twelve!
   (She turns to Rosie.) Is it me or he sleepwalking in there tonight?
ROSIE: He's keeping his usual pace. Slow as molasses in January.
NELL: What a night this is! You've got to check out table twelve. The suit
   with the slicked-back hair is breaking up with his girlfriend. Poor
   thing, she's been in tears since the salad coarse. What a dog!
   (Rosie looks off at the table in question, shaking her head, sympatheti-
   cally.)
ROSIE: Yeah, he brings his girlfriend to a nice restaurant and ends it in
   public, so she won't make a scene and scream at him.
NELL: I should help her out and *accidentally* drop the lasagna in his lap.
   What d'ya think? Wouldn't that be fun? "Oh, I'm so sorry, how clumsy
   of me! And all that hot oil and tomato sauce on your crotch!"
ROSIE: That's a brilliant idea. You can count on a big tip from that table!
NELL: Rosie, women have to stick together and help each other out. You
   know, like a sisterhood thing. Besides, I can tell looking at him, he's
   gonna be a lousy tipper. It's those shifty eyes of his. I'll be lucky to
   get ten percent!
   (Rosie laughs, and turns to the kitchen.)
ROSIE: *(Loudly.)* Arturo! I'm still here waiting, doll. Where are my soups
   for table five?
   (Turning back to Nell.) So, are you on tomorrow?
NELL: Yeah, how about you?
ROSIE: No. But Alex's got his family coming over for dinner, so I'm cooking, which is not my idea of a day off! My idea of a day off is being
   off my feet.
NELL: I'm sure Alex would be happy to help you there!
ROSIE: No, no, no. I don't want to be on my back or on my feet! I just
   wanna be on my *butt!* Sitting, watching TV, relaxing! My whole life

centers around food! I'm either serving it, cooking it, shopping for it or watching it!

NELL: Watching it?

ROSIE: Yeah! You know that saying: "You should watch what you eat?" Well, I watch it . . . and then I eat it!

(Nell glances over at her table quickly and yells out to the kitchen.)

NELL: Arturo? Are we waiting for the eggplant to be flown in from Italy?

(She raises her eyebrows and turns back to Rosie.)

NELL: He's getting a little testy, isn't he? He flipped me off again!

ROSIE: You just make him crazy. You're lucky he doesn't hit you with the frying pan! Alex does that to me when I'm cooking. I'm trying to get five things out of the oven, and he's sittin' there holding a beer, yammering on about work that day! The man truly has no idea how focused I have to be to turn out a good meal.

NELL: Please. Alex adores the ground you walk on.

ROSIE: *(Good naturedly.)* Yeah, well, it's a good thing he does! I've raised two sons and my husband! Taught them all manners and how to be polite to women!

NELL: Any chance I can send Barry your way and you can work on him for awhile?

ROSIE: Nell? Why are you still going out with him? I frankly think a guy his age whose mother still runs his life is damaged goods, if you know what I mean. I'd bail, if I were you.

NELL: Well, I'm keeping my options open! I check out every guy that comes into this restaurant. Problem is, they're usually with women, so I have to keep hanging around the table eavesdropping to get the skinny on their relationship! Usually, the girl starts giving me dirty looks though, so I have to pretend I'm checking on their breadbasket.

ROSIE: That would probably be more effective if you actually *had* some bread to offer them!

NELL: Good idea. I'll remember that!

ROSIE: *(Looking around.)* Hey, the ex-girlfriend at table twelve just jumped up and ran to the bathroom. Poor thing.

NELL: All right, I better go over there and see if he wants the check early. Maybe I can at least spill his water in his lap!

ROSIE: You go, girl!

(Nell walks off and Rosie turns her attention to the kitchen.)

ROSIE: Arturo, do you need me to come in there with a can opener for that soup? No! No! Don't you dare flip me off! I'll pour salt on your food and everyone will send it back! *(Throws her hands up.)* Ah, hell with it. I'm going out for a smoke.

(She walks off, waving at the kitchen.)

Notes to Sandra and Iris Scene

Hopefully an actress can have fun with Sandra's role, limited only by her imagination. Sandra is reactionary, opinionated, idiosyncratic, and socially obtuse. She has a very positive self-image, however, and seems to exist in a world unto herself.

She is determined to plan a vacation—ideally, one that entails no travelling or interaction with other human beings. Ironically, she doesn't recognize the conflict in those ambitions, and that sets the stage for Iris's dilemma.

Iris is a seasoned travel agent, confident in her ability to satisfy her client's itineraries, wherever their travels might take them. Ordinarily, Iris's demeanor is professional, upbeat, and accommodating, but Sandra drives her to distraction and ultimately Iris's only goal is to eject this woman from her office.

Audiences have responded very well to these characters, especially when the actress playing Iris uses expressive facial responses while keeping her dialogue subtle and underplayed. It contrasts beautifully with the intensity, quirkiness, and humor an actress should bring to Sandra's role.

SANDRA and IRIS

A travel agent and a prospective client discuss travel options.
Iris Willoughby, a travel agent, sits behind her desk, working. Sandra
Hess, a woman in her mid-twenties, enters.

IRIS: Miss Hess, please come in. Now, remind me again, who referred you to Global Travel?

SANDRA: *(Sitting down.)* Jim and Paula Rendell.

IRIS: Oh, yes. They went to the Bahamas. The Princess Cruise, Fiesta Deck, deluxe cabin. Lovely couple. How are they?

SANDRA: Divorced.

IRIS: Divorced? Already? The cruise was only six months ago.

SANDRA: Yeah, well, Jim had a few nasty secrets in his past. It wasn't pretty. Anyway, Paula's doing fine, cleaned him out, already seeing a new guy. I'm trying to remember his name, is it Steve? Maybe, Bill . . .

IRIS: *(Interrupting.)* How about if we discuss your travel plans? Now, what did we have in mind? A whirlwind tour of Europe? A Club-Med experience? Are we thinking a relaxing beach vacation?

SANDRA: We? Are you planning on joining me?

IRIS: What? Uh, no, I use "we" as a figure of speech. I certainly have no intention of accompanying you on your trip.

SANDRA: *(Relieved.)* Okay, good. I mean, I know I look young, but I don't need a chaperone or anything. You know, no offense, but I don't even know you. Who knows whether we'd even get along?
(Iris glances at Sandra, questioning her mental health.)

IRIS: Well, I'm glad we put that concern to rest. Now, are you interested in going abroad? Europe maybe?

SANDRA: No. I was there once, that was enough. It did nothing but rain, no one spoke English and their toilet paper is very abrasive. Altogether unpleasant.

IRIS: Uh-huh. Well, it doesn't sound like Europe is the answer. Perhaps you can tell me where you are interested in going.

SANDRA: See, that's the problem. I love the *idea* of traveling, I just don't like the traveling itself. You know, the whole physical act of traveling: the airports, the trains, whatever . . . A lot of time spent surrounded by too many people crowded together who smell bad! Haven't you found that to be the case? There are always those ones that don't use deodorant and they end up right next to you, don't they?

IRIS: *(A beat.)* That is unfortunate when that happens. Perhaps you should consider a road trip. Just you, alone, in your car, driving. Maybe Vermont? It's a lovely time of year to see the leaves change. Burlington is a charming little town with quaint . . .

SANDRA: *(Interrupting.)* No. I don't like driving. Nothing but traffic everywhere you go and you have to put up with bad drivers who tailgate or even worse than that, they sit along side you with their fingers in their nose! God, don't you hate that? It can ruin your whole day.

IRIS: Right, then. Let's eliminate that road trip idea. How about an island resort? Hawaii, maybe? There are so many beautiful hotels and beaches. A week in the sand and surf, relaxing and enjoying the balmy island breezes . . .

SANDRA: *(Wrinkles her nose.)* Geckos.

IRIS: Geckos?

SANDRA: Those little lizards that stick to the ceiling. Ugh!

IRIS: *(Smiling weakly.)* How about the Wine Country? Gorgeous landscapes, luxurious spas, over 300 magnificent wineries . . .

SANDRA: *(Points to her stomach.)* Indigestion. Wine gives me indigestion.

IRIS: Lake Tahoe, perhaps? Fabulous scenery, exciting nightlife, action-packed casinos . . .

SANDRA: *(Shaking her head.)* Three years in Gamblers Anonymous. Took me forever to pay off my debts.

(Iris regards this woman, nonplussed.)

IRIS: I don't seem to be doing too well. Maybe you could give me a list of places you don't want to visit, and I'll try to come up with some alternatives.

SANDRA: That could take me some time. I was hoping to . . .

(Iris stands up, walks around her desk and pulls Sandra out of her seat, escorting her to the door of her office.)

IRIS: You work on that list tonight and call me first thing in the morning!

SANDRA: You know, maybe you joining me on my vacation wouldn't be such a bad idea. I'm easygoing, lots of fun, and a real magnet for guys! *(Chuckling.)* They just love my sunny disposition! Anyway, give it some thought.

IRIS: *(Horrified.)* What a sweet offer, thank you. Bye, bye.

(Iris closes the door behind Sandra and immediately returns to her desk. She buzzes her secretary and speaks to the intercom.)

IRIS: Marie, when that woman Sandra Hess calls tomorrow, tell her I took an indefinite leave of absence. Recommend Travel Dot Com or whatever the hell that William Shatner endorses. In fact, try to find his home phone and suggest she consider taking him on her trip!

WOMEN

❖ ❖ ❖

drama

Notes to Mel and Lynn Scene

Mel and Lynn have been friends for twenty years. They can always count on each other for support through thick and thin. Through the years, the two couples have taken vacations together and socialized regularly. Unlike some situations, where couples have divided loyalty when their friends separate, Lynn and her husband, George, are equally devoted to Mel and outraged by her husband's behavior.

In this scene, Mel talks to Lynn with great candor about her conflict. She has spent months trying to come to terms with her husband's betrayal and her feelings of anger, sorrow and disillusionment. Now faced with the prospect of taking him back, she questions whether the damage done to the marriage is irreparable.

Lynn loves Mel like a sister and feels great empathy for her turmoil. She is a supportive friend and knows that her role is not to offer judgement but to be a sounding board for Mel to sort out her conflicting emotions.

MEL and LYNN

Two old friends in their forties discuss marriage, infidelity, family and dignity.
Mel opens the door of her house and her friend Lynn, charges in.

LYNN: Scott wants to come back home?

MEL: He called me this morning.

LYNN: Didn't I tell you this would happen? I knew he'd come to his senses!

MEL: I'm beyond thinking he *has* any sense at this point, the bastard.

LYNN: What did you say? Are you going to take him back?

MEL: *(A beat.)* I don't know. I need some time to think about it.

LYNN: Do you still want him?

MEL: I shouldn't . . . If I had an ounce of dignity, I would have hung up on him.

LYNN: Mel, come on. You guys had a good marriage for a long time. It would be pretty irrational to not even consider giving him another chance.

MEL: Oh, please. Was it rational of him to leave me for a twenty-two-year-old named Honey? Honey isn't the name of a person, it's the name of a lipgloss! For Christ's sakes, the sonavobitch walked out on me and our two kids so he could diddle some airhead who works at the cosmetic counter of Bloomingdales!

LYNN: I know, I'm just saying that . . .

MEL: What? If George had walked out on you, you would have shot him in his tracks.

LYNN: That's true and he knows it. It's probably the only reason he hasn't cheated on me with some nineteen-year-old blonde.
(Mel sits down and Lynn sits next to her.)

MEL: I've asked myself for the last two months what this girl could have offered him that he was willing to throw away a marriage for. We shared twenty years of experience and the bond of two children. Are those things so dispensable that a man discards them for some babe with a flat stomach and a perfect butt?

LYNN: Why don't you ask Scott that question?

MEL: I did! I asked him this morning. He went into some sob story about his mid-life crisis and losing himself amid all his confusion, blah, blah, blah . . . It was so trite, I nearly vomited.

LYNN: Do you think there's any truth to it? I mean, did you see any signs of a midlife crisis before this all happened?

MEL: Not that I was aware of. But who the hell knows? I thought I knew him inside and out, but obviously I was deluding myself. The man I knew would never have done this, so I'm not sure who he is at this point.

LYNN: Honey, this has gotta be so hard on you. I don't know what I'd do if I were in your shoes.

MEL: Lynnie, I don't know if I can ever trust him again. And without that, how do you live with someone day to day? I have to decide what's the best decision not just for me, but for my kids.

LYNN: Well, there's no doubt that Jeff and Lisa want him home, is there?

MEL: It's more than that. It's what kind of example do I set by taking him back? What does that say to my son? That it's okay to be unfaithful? That commitment and loyalty don't really matter much in a marriage? What about my daughter? Do I teach her that a woman allows herself to be discarded and humiliated?

LYNN: No, of course not. But on the other hand, you can teach them a lesson about human frailty and forgiveness.

MEL: Yes, but I'd actually have to feel forgiving, which at this point, I don't.

LYNN: Mel, you don't have to take this all on yourself. Scott's the one that has a lot of explaining to do to your children.

MEL: That's true, but in spite of them wanting him back, they're both so angry with him that they haven't been willing to even see him since he left.

LYNN: Nor have George and I for that matter.

MEL: He called you two? Why didn't you tell me?

LYNN: Because I knew it would upset you. Besides, I summarily told him what a raving asshole we thought he was and that was pretty much the end of that.

MEL: I can always count on you!

LYNN: You better believe it.

(Mel leans over and hugs Lynn, kissing her on the cheek.)

(Jenna rolls her eyes, and they exchange a half-hearted smile.)
JENNA: I'll be back in a while.
   (She walks out the door, and Kate sits down, wearily massaging her temples.)

Notes to Sheila and Melissa Scene

These are women of different generations. How they lead their lives, what they value, and who they are, is in constant conflict!

Sheila loves her daughter, but rather than being proud of her daughter's accomplishments—becoming a veterinarian, buying her own home, being independent and self-sufficient—she only focuses on what she believes is her daughter's abnormal and pathetic single life.

Sheila's whole existence is being a wife. She has married five times and believes that all women should marry, dedicate their lives to their husbands and bear children. No doubt Melissa's choice to pursue a career and not marry is due in large part to her desire to be *nothing* like her mother. That fact is a constant slap in the face to Sheila. She wants the best for her daughter, but according to *her* vision of what's best.

Melissa loves her mother, and is tolerant of her antics and efforts at manipulation. She recognizes that her mother will never change, will never stop needling her, and will never truly treat her like an adult. Her mother will use guilt, prodding, whatever it takes, to try and mold her daughter into her image.

The actresses in this scene should capitalize on the differences in their characters. Sheila's emotions are broader, bigger, and more dramatic. Melissa is grounded, matter-of-fact, more accepting of her mother than her mother is of her. She recognizes that her mother will never change and the only chance they have for peace between them is if she takes it all with a sense of humor and lets it roll off her back.

SHEILA and MELISSA

A woman comes to visit her daughter for the weekend and volunteers endless opinions about what's missing in her daughter's life.

Melissa, a down-to-earth, thirty-five-year-old woman, enters her house with her mother, Sheila, a coifed, overdressed woman in her late fifties.

MELISSA: Come on in, Ma.

SHEILA: *(Scanning the room.)* Melissa, this house is darling!

MELISSA: C'mon, I'll show you around.

SHEILA: Honey, gimme a minute to sit down. These pumps are killing me.

MELISSA: Why won't you wear flats when you're traveling?

SHEILA: Don't be ridiculous. I live in heels. I got these to match the dress I wore to the funeral, as a matter of fact. Which, if you had been there, you would have known.

MELISSA: I told you I was working. I couldn't take the time off.

SHEILA: So you said. It wasn't easy for me, you know. Losing my husband, the love of my life!

MELISSA: Mother, Harry was not the love of your life! You had only been married to the man for eight months.

SHEILA: Well, as it happens, I loved him dearly. I thought I would spend the rest of my life with him.

MELISSA: Yeah. That's what you said about the last four men you were married to.

SHEILA: *(Indignant.)* I enter into every marriage with the highest hopes! Unlike you, I might add, who refuses to walk down the aisle even once!

MELISSA: *(Looking at her watch.)* We didn't even make it through one hour without you starting in.

SHEILA: Don't take that tone with me, Missy.

MELISSA: Ma. Let's have a nice weekend without arguing. Unpack and relax for a while. I'll run over to the clinic to pick up your grandson who is being groomed, just for your benefit.

SHEILA: Oh, for God's sake, Barney is not my grandson! If I had a grandson, he would be cute and cuddly, not walking around on four legs drooling!

MELISSA: It's Barkley, and he's a golden retriever, he does not drool!

SHEILA: Whatever! You're a thirty-five-year-old woman who lives with a dog! You should be living with a husband and a child.

MELISSA: According to you! I'm in no rush, mother. I do not have a biological clock ticking inside me, urging me to marry and procreate.

SHEILA: Well, you should. According to Dr. Goldman, you don't have that many years left.

MELISSA: Who the hell is Dr. Goldman?

SHEILA: My gynecologist! He says women over forty have a very tough time getting pregnant.

MELISSA: Mother, women can have children well into their forties. I'm not worried about it.

SHEILA: Well, I am! You're a smart and pretty girl. You've had lots of opportunities to settle down with a nice man, but you've chosen not to. I just don't understand. It's not natural to prefer being alone!

MELISSA: Ma, I love my life, I really do. I love being a Vet and working with animals. I work long hours and when I come home to this house, I love the solitude and quiet. I make dinner, I play music, and I relax. I'm happy.

SHEILA: Imagine how much happier you'd be if you had a man to share it with.

MELISSA: Mother, I'm not you! I don't need a man to complete my life. I have friends, I socialize when I want to, and I even date from time to time!

SHEILA: It's my fault, isn't it? If you hadn't been an only child, you would have learned how to share your life. People are meant to share their lives.

MELISSA: I'll be happy to share my life when I find a man worth sharing it with!

SHEILA: Well, if you haven't found one man up to your standards, perhaps your standards are too high!

MELISSA: And maybe yours are too low! You've married men you had nothing in common with! Men who had no redeemable qualities other than their willingness to support you!

(Sheila recoils. She turns away from Melissa and straightens her skirt.)

MELISSA: Ma, I'm sorry. I had no right to say that.

SHEILA: Do you *try* to hurt me, or does it just happen?

MELISSA: I never mean to hurt you. I get defensive! You attack the choices I've made in my life, with no respect to the fact that I'm a different woman than you!

SHEILA: Yes you are, and I think you revel in that fact. *(A beat.)* Let me tell you something Missy; I don't regret not having a career. My career is being a wife! I've loved every minute of being Mrs. Sheila Rivers-Whitman-Daly-Grotha-Morgan!

MELISSA: *(Gentle.)* I know you have. And I'm sure you'll add another man's name to that list before the year is out.

SHEILA: *(Smiling in spite of herself.)* As it happens, I met a very attractive widower on the plane and I'm having dinner with him tomorrow night.

MELISSA: Tomorrow night? I thought you came out here to see me!

SHEILA: Oh please! By then you'll be thrilled to get me out of the house. You and Barkley can enjoy a quiet evening together.

MELISSA: *(Rolls her eyes and smiles.)* I'll go get your luggage.

Notes to Carol and Louise Scene

Carol and Louise both teach junior high school, but their perspective on teaching is very different. Carol has lost her enthusiasm for teaching and wrestles with the frustration of her life and career. Louise has taught for twenty years, and still relishes the opportunity to inspire students with knowledge. Having survived cancer years ago, she embraces each day as a gift.

The tone of this scene between Carol and Louise is both conversational and heartfelt.

They've interacted more as co-workers than intimate friends, but they're fond of each other. Carol respects Louise's judgement and confides in her, hoping to make sense of her quandary.

Through the course of the conversation, both women reveal more about themselves than they have previously shared, and their honesty strengthens their friendship.

Carol is reserved by nature, hesitant to change her life, yet aware that she needs to pursue new challenges and find passion in both her professional and social life.

Louise's positive nature is reflected in her teaching, her friendships and her outlook on life. When she talks about her bout with cancer, she speaks without self-pity or drama. Her reference to it is a way of explaining her advice to Carol about embracing opportunity and not letting fear stand in her way.

CAROL and LOUISE

Two teachers sit together on a bench during lunch hour, discussing their respective views on life. Carol is thirty-five, reflective and soft-spoken. Louise is fifty, good-natured and upbeat.

CAROL: Do you ever think about quitting?

LOUISE: No, why? Are you thinking about it?

CAROL: I am, actually.

LOUISE: What else would you do?

CAROL: I'm not sure. That's the problem.

LOUISE: That's not a problem, it's a challenge.

CAROL: Right. By the time I go back to college, get a different degree, another job, and start earning a decent salary, I'll be forty.

LOUISE: Honey, in five years you'll be forty, either way. Difference is, you'll be forty with a new career or without one.

CAROL: *(Smiling.)* That's one way to look at it. When I started teaching ten years ago, I really loved it. I did, I thought it was a noble profession. I don't feel that way anymore. Do you still love it?

LOUISE: I do. I still love teaching students. I think teachers are unsung heroes. We can change a child's mind and shape their futures. When I see even one kid get excited about learning, I'm thrilled!

CAROL: I forgot how repulsively optimistic you are.

LOUISE: I know. It drives the kids crazy!

CAROL: Maybe I'm just burnt out. Everyday I feel like I'm knocking my head against the blackboard trying to get these kids to care about what I'm teaching them.

LOUISE: Well, maybe you *should* quit then. If you're fed-up, you're not doing anyone a favor. You or the students. What about changing schools? You think working at a private school would make a difference?

CAROL: Not really. Probably the only benefit would be not spending as much time wondering whether every kid has a gun in his backpack.

LOUISE: It horrifies me that we even have to consider that possibility.

CAROL: Well, we do, like it or not.

LOUISE: Between the drugs and the violence, it's out of control.

CAROL: You know, I keep thinking about having kids myself, but the prospect scares me.

LOUISE: You'd be a great mother. Maybe part of your frustration is that you spend all day around everyone else's kids, and not your own. Your biological clock is ticking and you need to answer the call.

CAROL: Right, that's the answer! I'll forget about pursuing a lofty and rewarding career and settle down and raise a passel of brats.

LOUISE: Don't kid yourself, you'd probably love it.

CAROL: Maybe, but I think I'd need some male companionship to help me out there.

LOUISE: No prospects?

CAROL: Not one. I actually had a moment last week where I was considering Barry Premus. Can you imagine that? He came blowing into the faculty lounge in his tracksuit and silver whistle and I found myself admiring his bravado.

LOUISE: Carol, you are in trouble. That guy has way too much alpha male in him to be good for any woman. In the middle of a date he'd probably tell you to drop to the floor and give him twenty push-ups! You've got to rethink that choice.

CAROL: It was a weak moment, what can I say?

(Louise smiles at Carol and pats her arm.)

LOUISE: Don't let yourself settle for less than what you deserve.

CAROL: I'm afraid that's just what I'm doing. I see myself running in place and I can't figure out why. Am I too young to be having a mid-life crisis?

LOUISE: Hell, yes! But all the same, life's too short to spend your days being discontent, and if that's where you are, you need to shake things up. Move on in your life. Find your passion!

CAROL: I'm trying! It just isn't so easy to find!

(Louise chuckles, then pauses a moment before speaking.)

LOUISE: Let me tell you something. When I was your age, I wanted to conquer the world, and nothing was getting in my way. *(A beat.)* I got ovarian cancer, and had to reevaluate what I was gonna conquer.

CAROL: *(Stunned.)* My God. Why didn't you ever tell me this before?

LOUISE: *(Smiling.)* There was never a need to tell you before. I'm telling you now, because it taught me some wonderful things about life. I survived it, and I feel blessed because of it! Don't stop yourself from pursuing anything or everything. It's all within your reach, trust me.

CAROL: *(Heartfelt.)* You're an inspiration.

LOUISE: Why the hell do you think I'm such a good teacher!

(Carol drapes her arm over Louise's shoulder, and they head back to their classrooms.)

MEN

❖ ❖ ❖

comedy

Notes to Patrick and Sean Scene

Patrick and Sean have been friends since childhood. They grew up in the same neighborhood, went to the same schools, and are now at an age where their lives will take them in different directions.

Patrick's childhood was tumultuous with alcoholic parents, and he spent more of his time at Sean's house than at his own. Sean's mother made Patrick feel like a member of her own family, and he was a welcomed guest at their dinner table every week.

The scene is generally humorous, but there are layers of unspoken drama that underscore the comedy between these two friends. Sean has the opportunity to move to Chicago and explore a new future, but feels badly about leaving his friend behind. In a moment of enthusiasm, he tries to talk Patrick into joining him, but Patrick's sense of obligation to his mother prevents him from pursuing a future of his own. Sean immediately realizes he shouldn't have pressed the issue and should have been more sensitive to Patrick's situation.

They exchange several honest admissions through the scene, but the characters try to mask their vulnerability in bravado and humor. The actors playing the scene should communicate both the humor of their good-natured ribbing as well as the dramatic beats when Patrick discusses his family and Sean acknowledges his discomfort being compared to his successful brothers.

PATRICK and SEAN

Sean and Patrick, twenty-two-year-old friends, sit in a bar discussing women, careers and family.

SEAN: . . . Anyway, she asked me what I was gonna do with my life and I told her I had no idea.

PATRICK: What? She thinks you should have it all mapped out already?

SEAN: *(Sarcastic.)* C'mon, man, you know my mother. In sixth grade, she started showing me college brochures! She's a woman who believes in planning ahead.

PATRICK: Look at it this way: Eileen's got six sons, all of which have made her proud and she's not going to let the youngest one disgrace her. Admit it, Bud, you're the black sheep of the family!

SEAN: No! Everyone else is an over-achiever. Michael's a lawyer, Riley's an architect, Tommy's in med-school, Brian's a stockbroker and Aidan's first novel made the best-seller list. No pressure to compete, there! *(Patrick smirks at Sean's familiar lament.)*

PATRICK: Hey, no one in your family has succeeded in porno. If God had been kinder to you, you could have given that a shot and become a real star!

SEAN: God's been plenty good to me, pal. I don't hear Jennifer complaining.

PATRICK: Ah, what does she know? Poor girl, she could have had me and got stuck with you. She's gonna spend the rest of her life regretting that choice!

SEAN: *(Laughing)* Right! Your first date you got drunk and suavely puked on her on the way home. I'm sure she was pining away for you after that illustrious evening!

PATRICK: Listen, she was hot for me, there's no doubt about it. Then you swooped in and she never knew what hit her. The Sean O'Malley curse! I should never have forgiven you for that serious breach of friendship.

SEAN: You love that horseshit story! I didn't ask her out for a month after you crashed and burned. And by the way, she wasn't interested in you even before you hurled!

PATRICK: *(Grinning.)* She lies! The woman wanted me to father her children, and probably still does.

SEAN: Speaking of women, how's Beth treatin' you?

PATRICK: No complaints. She laughs at my jokes, puts out regularly and plays a mean game of pool. She may be the world's best girlfriend! Even my mother likes her, imagine that.

SEAN: *(Serious.)* How is your ma? Is she still off the sauce?

PATRICK: For the moment. You know, it never lasts long. Since my dad died, she's drinking a little less, but it's day to day. She's always callin' me, bitching about my not visiting her often enough.

SEAN: I know it's hard on you, man. *(Uneasy.)* Listen Pat, I wanted to talk to you about something.

PATRICK: What's goin' on?

SEAN: Jennifer got that job in Chicago. She's moving this month and I'm thinking of going with her.

PATRICK: You're serious? You're gonna leave behind all your friends? And what about your folks? They'll go ballistic.

SEAN: Hey, I'm not letting my parents decide what I do with my life. And I hear Chicago's got a lot of job opportunities. I can get into some career without being compared to my brothers.

PATRICK: That's worth something. You're not gonna become a Bulls fan, are you?

SEAN: Oh, fuck that!

PATRICK: That makes me feel a little better.

SEAN: Listen, Pat, why don't you come with me? We could both get great jobs, earn some dough and get into bar fights rooting for the Knicks on TV!

PATRICK: Yeah, well, tempting as that sounds, I'll pass. I'd end up moving in with you, Jennifer would throw herself at me . . . It would get ugly.

SEAN: In your dreams, dirtbag! C'mon, I'm serious, think about it.
(Patrick smiles at his friend, then slowly the smile fades.)

PATRICK: I can't. You know I can't.

SEAN: Your mom?

PATRICK: Yeah. Someone's gotta look after her. She didn't have it easy with my dad. She took a lotta beatings from that bastard. I owe it to her.

SEAN: Sure. Of course.

(They both shift, uncomfortably. Sean attempts to lighten the mood.)

SEAN: Hey, you know I'll be back to visit all the time.

PATRICK: No doubt. You won't last a month without me! *(He stands up.)* I'm going up to the bar to get us a few beers.

SEAN: *(Feigned shock.) You're* paying?

PATRICK: It's a day of surprises. What can I say?

Notes to Dennis and Zach Scene

This scene depends on the different rhythms of the two characters. They're both in the maternity ward, awaiting the birth of their child, but their responses to that event are very dissimilar.

Zach is a nervous wreck, a man so overwhelmed by the concept of parenting that he's come unglued. He's both thrilled and petrified, and his head is whirling like a spin cycle.

Dennis, on the other hand, couldn't be calmer or more relaxed. He's had several children already and takes it all in stride.

Throughout the scene, Zach's physical actions mirror his psychological hysteria: pacing, biting his cuticles, tugging on his hair, etc . . . All the while, Dennis sits calmly in his chair, his eyes following Zach like he's watching a tennis match. Dennis attempts to calm Zach down with words of support and advice, being both sympathetic and amused by this man's nervous agitation.

DENNIS and ZACH

Two men meet in the waiting room of a maternity ward.
Dennis, a man in his late forties, sits calmly reading a newspaper and
glancing at Zach, a wiry thirty-year-old, pacing nervously back and forth.

DENNIS: Is this your first?

ZACH: What?

DENNIS: Your first baby?

ZACH: Oh, yeah. Is it that obvious?

DENNIS: I know the signs.

ZACH: How about you?

DENNIS: Oh no. This is our fifth. I'm an old pro.

ZACH: Your fifth? My God, that's a lot of kids!

DENNIS: That it is. This is our last though. My wife told me after this
one, I either had to get a vasectomy or never touch her again!

ZACH: That's brutal.

DENNIS: *(Laughing.)* You can say that again. And I'll tell ya, on certain
days I'm not sure which is the worse of two evils!

ZACH: How do you survive five kids? I'm panicked about one. I was just
in there with my wife, helping her with the Lamaze thing, you know,
breathe, breathe, push, push . . . I started to hyperventilate and passed
out on the floor.

DENNIS: That had to be embarrassing.

ZACH: It was humiliating! They had to tell me to step outside and get
some air.

DENNIS: Listen, you're not the first guy to take a dive in the delivery room,
don't worry about it.

ZACH: You think? My poor wife is trying to push something the size of
a basketball out of her and she's fine. I breathe heavy and collapse.

DENNIS: Do you know whether it's a girl or a boy?

ZACH: A girl. How 'bout you?

DENNIS: We're having a girl too. We already have two boys and two girls.
David, Della, Danny and Debra. This one we're naming Deanne.

ZACH: That's a lot of D's to remember.

DENNIS: Yep! And my wife's name is Dorothy and I'm Dennis.

ZACH: Nice to meet you, Dennis. I'm Zach.

(They shake hands and Zach continues pacing.)

ZACH: Can I ask you something? How do you prepare for this? I mean, really? How do you know you'll be a good parent? What if you're not and the kid hates you and runs away from home at thirteen to join a cult?

DENNIS: You gotta get ahold of yourself, man. Are you always this nervous?

ZACH: No . . . I don't think so.

DENNIS: Well, there's hope for you then. Relax! Nobody's prepared for having kids the first time. You're exhausted the first year, but you manage.

ZACH: So you're not so tired that you forget to feed 'em? Or put them in the bath water and they shrivel up like a prune, cause you fell asleep yourself?

DENNIS: No. They're not like house keys. You don't put them down and hours later try to remember where you left them.

ZACH: Right. Of course not. *(He inhales and exhales.)* I gotta calm down. I've been so wound up, I'm pulling my hair out. I think I've got a bald spot the size of a quarter!

DENNIS: Look, kids don't come with manuals. You love 'em, protect 'em and teach 'em right from wrong. Sometimes they test your patience and make you nuts, but when you tuck them into bed and they kiss you goodnight, you could die a happy man.

ZACH: *(Smiling for the first time.)* Yeah?

DENNIS: My hand to God! And here's a good tip; when your daughter's a teenager, invite her date in when he picks her up. Pat him on the back, give him a big smile, shake his hand and squeeze so hard you crush his grip. It works like a charm! Turns the punk into a choirboy and he drops her off without even a kiss on the cheek!

ZACH: I like that!

DENNIS: Trust me, parenting is a creative skill.

ZACH: Okay, I better get in there. I'm ready.

DENNIS: Ah, Zach . . . you might wanna zip up your fly before you go into the delivery room.

(Zach looks down, embarrassed, and yanks his zipper up.)

ZACH: Thanks! I would have hated that being my daughter's first memory of me!

(Zach bumps his head as he charges out the door. Dennis rolls his eyes, chuckling, and returns to his newspaper.)

Notes to Mickey and Evan Scene

Mickey and Evan are both in their late twenties, starving writers, aspiring novelists, and good friends. They work at night waiting tables and spend their days trying to finish a novel, which they're convinced will end up on the best-seller list.

Mickey is the more hyper of the two, more driven and animated. Evan tends to be more of a slacker with a dryer wit and a calmer disposition. They work well together, and the have the ability to feed off each other's ideas and communicate on the same wavelength.

Mickey and Evan met years ago, working the same shift at Kinko's. Neither has much luck with women, but they're hopeful a successful novel will rectify that problem.

The scene depends on a natural flow between these two characters. They can finish each other's sentences, but their rhythm is very different. In order for the dialogue not to run together, it's important that Evan's slower pacing offsets Mickey's intense energy.

Evan pauses occasionally before responding, partially because he's lost in thought, partially because he's timing a retort guaranteed to infuriate Mickey. Mickey's brain runs at full speed, as does his mouth and imagination. He's bright, irreverent, and impatient. Evan knows just how to goad him, and it drives Mickey to distraction.

MICKEY and EVAN

Two frustrated writers discuss a potential story idea.
Mickey, a disheveled twenty-eight-year-old sits alone at a coffeehouse, impatiently tapping his foot. Moments later his friend, Evan, enters and joins him at the table.

MICKEY: Nice of you to show up, dude. Did I not say four o'clock? Coulda sworn I said four o'clock.

EVAN: Jesus, take a Valium, Mick! I'm only ten minutes late. *(He notices empty coffee cups on the table.)* Oh, never mind. Two double shots of Expresso, no wonder you're cranked!

MICKEY: I'm not cranked! I'm alert and chemically enhanced.

EVAN: Yeah. So are you gonna tell me why I had to rush over here?

MICKEY: Very promising news. Janis hooked us up with her editor at *LA Magazine* and he's interested in us doing a freelance piece about coffeehouses.

EVAN: You gotta be kidding me. You're excited about doing a fluff piece on caffeinated beverages? At least I have some creative integrity . . .

MICKEY: *(Interrupting.)* 1000 words. Seven hundred bucks.

EVAN: I'm in! So, what's your take on the article?

MICKEY: It's very simple, look around you. Every square block in LA has a coffeehouse, right? Starbucks, The Coffee Bean, Peet's Coffee . . .

EVAN: What's the point?

MICKEY: Irrespective of time of day, they're all teeming with people. This naturally begs the question, "Who are all these fucking people and why don't any of them have jobs?"

EVAN: I like that! I've asked myself that same question, even though we are the very people you're describing!

MICKEY: Exactly! And who better to write the article than us? Anyway, we come up with some answers.

EVAN: So, Latte-sipping, unemployed actors, with beepers and cel-phones is probably too easy an answer?

MICKEY: You are a simpleton, and I'm embarrassed to call you my partner.

EVAN: *(Dry.)* Get over it. The truth will set you free.

MICKEY: I'm gonna get another coffee.

EVAN: No more coffee! You're about to levitate as it is.

MICKEY: All right, what about this? Maybe the whole phenomenon of coffeehouses is an answer for a generation of people who've given up excess drugs and alcohol and want somewhere to hang out that provides a legally stimulating substance.

EVAN: Or, it's a gathering spot for people whose lives are becoming more isolated and lonely. You know, computer geeks.

MICKEY: Maybe it's just the last place a person can sit and smoke cigarettes without fear of condemnation.

EVAN: Ohhh, condemnation! Very impressive word, they'll love that.

MICKEY: *(Ignoring him.)* Okay, but understanding why flocks of people drink their daily dose of coffee at these places still doesn't answer the question of: Why does everyone have the free time to be there?

EVAN: Boredom?

(Mickey glares, disgustedly.)

EVAN: Jesus, Mick. Lighten up! Maybe it's not that all these people across LA are truly unemployed, but rather, they're self-employed. How's that?

MICKEY: Yeah, so they're what? Screenwriters? Personal trainers?

EVAN: Freelance photographers, novelists. That's us, self-employed novelists! Has a nice ring to it, doesn't it?

MICKEY: Helluva lot better than starving, pathetic writers . . . Okay, so they're self-employed. Maybe they're internet-dot.com entrepreneurs. Creative, momentarily blocked souls looking for a jolt of inspiration.

EVAN: Maybe on a daily basis we're witnessing the creation of masterpieces. Maybe the future Bill Gates is coming up with the idea for the new Microsoft at Cyber Java on Hollywood Blvd . . .

MICKEY: Or maybe if F. Scott Fitzgerald were alive, he'd be writing *The Great Gatsby* at Urth Caffe on Melrose.

EVAN: Okay, but we know for a fact that Hemingway would still be on a barstool, right? No way I'm theorizing that Hemingway would be at Stonewalls in Brentwood.

MICKEY: *(Solemn.)* Absolutely. No chance of that.

(Mickey notices that Evan is starring off in the distance.)

MICKEY: Hello! What? Am I boring you?

EVAN: Huh? Oh, sorry. I was checking out the rack on that blonde in the corner. The sight of her elevated my whole day!

(Mickey cranes his neck and eyes the blonde, nodding in approval.)

MICKEY: Very nice. I could do with less makeup, but all in all, a good sighting.

(They take a moment in their reverie, then return to their conversation.)

EVAN: Where were we? Oh yeah. We could do a bunch of these articles. Cover all the social scenes happening in town. You know, yoga classes, cigar bars . . .

MICKEY: Nobody goes to cigar bars anymore. That's totally over.

EVAN: What are you talkin' about? Everybody still goes, don't they?

MICKEY: Thing of the past. You have got to get out more often, man.

(Mickey stands up and heads toward the door, Evan following behind.)

EVAN: I get out plenty.

MICKEY: No you don't. You're a total loser.

EVAN: Shut up! Are we writing at my place or yours?

MICKEY: Let's go to yours. My computer sucks.

EVAN: Okay . . .

MICKEY: You got coffee at your place?

EVAN: No more coffee!

Notes to Martin and Ted Scene

Martin Sullivan is a very cunning, opportunistic young man. During his tenure at an investment firm, he made it his business to keep his ear to the door and take notes on all the transactions he overheard. During that period of time, his boss engaged in insider trading with several friends of his and ultimately was convicted by the SEC. One of the friends he divulged information to was Ted Gross, a man careful enough to cover his tracks and avoid prosecution. Martin Sullivan discovered this information and has spent months trying to figure out how to use it to his advantage.

Martin moved to Los Angeles from Enid, Oklahoma, with dreams of fast women, fast cars and fast money. By nature he's a hustler and isn't interested in working his way to the top. He's been able to connive his way through life and feels entitled to all he can amass through his manipulation. What he neglects to realize in this interaction with Ted Gross is that he's out of his league. He's confident that his information gives him a winning hand, but Ted is more artful at deceit than he is and ultimately will figure out a way to undermine his plans.

Ted is a very clever and confident man, patronizing and self-important. In this scene, his dialogue is delivered very pointedly, and although he is momentarily unsettled by Martin's threats, he makes every effort to veil his distress. This young man presents a considerable concern, but Ted is sure he'll get the upper hand and control the damage, enjoying the opportunity to cut this kid down to size.

Martin begins the scene, attempting to be ingenuous and complimentary. He works his way up to threatening Ted, but continues to do it with a smile. Everything about his delivery has been rehearsed in front of a mirror, and he carries it off with unruffled confidence. When Ted accuses him of being Sammy Glick, Martin actually thinks Ted is impressed by him. The reference to *What Makes Sammy Run?* is Budd Schulberg's infamous novel, the title character being an unscrupulous young man in the film business with an insatiable appetite for success and no moral compass. Ted's reference is meant as anything but a compliment.

I hope the actors portraying these roles explore the many interpretations they can bring to these two cunning characters. I have seen it performed in very different ways and each time I was intrigued by the actors' choices and how they impacted Ted and Martin's interaction.

MARTIN and TED

An interview between the vice president of a resource management group and a crafty young trainee applying for a job.

Ted Gross, an imposing middle-age executive, sits at his desk opposite Martin Sullivan, a cocky twenty-five-year-old. Ted glances through Martin's resume.

TED: So you worked in the trainee programs at Paine-Webber and Merrill Lynch?

MARTIN: I sure did. I knew pretty quickly though, that neither place was right for me.

TED: You felt qualified to make that informed decision after three months?

MARTIN: Absolutely. I knew I wanted to be here, at Wilson-Gross. Your firm has a stellar reputation and I wanted to train under you. You're the man I want to learn from.

TED: Mr. Sullivan, sucking up to me is not going to get you the job.

MARTIN: *(Guffaws.)* Of course not! I'm just happy to be here. It's taken me six months to get this interview.

TED: I'm a busy man.

MARTIN: No doubt! I used to work at Haney, Mills and Stoppard and I constantly heard your name mentioned as the one man that they wanted to steal away for their firm!

TED: *(Flinches.)* You worked at Haney, Mills and Stoppard? Why isn't that on your resume?

MARTIN: *(Leans in confidentially.)* Well, after the SEC convicted Dick Haney on three counts, their reputation was pretty tainted. I didn't think it would serve me well!

TED: How prudent of you.

MARTIN: I think being circumspect is always wise. I know you'd agree.

TED: What exactly do you mean by that?

MARTIN: Just that I know you're very careful about how and who you do business with. Successful and wealthy men like you don't get that way by accident.

TED: *(Staring intently.)* What exactly was your position with HMS? A trainee?

MARTIN: Well, actually I worked directly for Dick Haney for a month when his assistant was ill. Just before he was arrested, in fact.

TED: I see.

MARTIN: I was able to learn a lot from him. If nothing else, just overhearing conversations, listening to his recommendations. I always say, the more you know, the better off you are!

TED: *(Coldly.)* Not necessarily.

MARTIN: I remember being amazed that he was willing to share that Nexon tip, boy! Apparently, the only ones that didn't take the fall with him were those smart enough to hide the money in offshore accounts.

TED: You have no idea what you're talking about.

MARTIN: *(Pointed.)* Actually, you'd be surprised what I know. I was responsible for shredding a lot of documents.

TED: *(Snide laughter.)* You wily little bastard! You thought you'd waltz in here and try to blackmail me?

MARTIN: Absolutely not! The thought never crossed my mind. Well, maybe for a second, but . . .

TED: Whatever you think you know, you don't!

MARTIN: *(Unctuous.)* Ted, I'm not interested in bringing you any harm. I take my hat off to you! You're a very clever man and working alongside you would be the best opportunity in the world for me.

TED: Don't ever call me Ted! You refer to me as Mr. Gross!

MARTIN: Sorry! I wasn't trying to be impertinent. I just see us becoming good friends.

TED: Let's cut the bullshit. What is it exactly you want?

MARTIN: I want to work for you. I want to learn all about the market and become a wealthy man myself. I see myself becoming a top financial advisor in no time!

TED: My God. You're Sammy Glick incarnate.

MARTIN: Thank you! I take that as a compliment. *What Makes Sammy Run* is one of my favorite books. He's a personal hero to me!

TED: Why doesn't that surprise me?

MARTIN: *(Ignoring the insult.)* So. Should we talk about a starting salary?

TED: We're not going to talk about anything.

MARTIN: I understand you have a lot to think about. I would just hate to see you take too long.

TED: Is that a veiled threat, you little putz?

MARTIN: Of course not! I'm just confident that you know your competition might steal me away, and I bring a lot of information to the job! *(Ted's eyes narrow.)*

TED: Don't think I'm not gonna have you checked out. I'll know everything about you down to the size of your shorts.

MARTIN: *(Smug.)* I'd be disappointed if you didn't, Ted.

(Martin smiles broadly and walks out the door, leaving Ted twitching in his chair.)

MEN

❖ ❖ ❖

drama

Notes to Samuel and Eli Scene

Actors have responded very positively to this scene, enjoying the opportunity to explore the exchange between these two characters.

Samuel and Eli have a good relationship as father and son, but the difference in their generations separates their sensibilities and viewpoints on life.

Samuel sees himself as an honest, hardworking man, a loving husband and supportive father. He took over his family's metal supply business when he was a young man and never had the opportunity to go to college. He was thrilled to be able to send Eli to Princeton and took great pride in his son's academic accomplishments, but he feels the time has come for Eli to settle down and commit to a career.

Eli is about to turn thirty and is at a crossroad in his life, wrestling with the commitment of marriage and a lifelong career. He spent his childhood watching his father work day in and day out, never taking time off to attend Eli's sporting events or take the family on a vacation. He has great respect for his father but doesn't want to emulate his life. What he does aspire to is the lasting love his parents have sustained through the years.

The tone in this scene is confrontational, with both becoming defensive about the judgments they feel the other is making, but there is no genuine malice in their words. They each have strength in their convictions, and it makes for a heated argument; however, by the end of the scene, the wisdom in Samuel's advice reminds Eli of all that he admires about his father.

SAMUEL and ELI

A Father and Son discuss commitments about marriage and career. Samuel is working at his desk. His son, Eli, enters and looks at his father for a moment before speaking.

ELI: Dad. You have a minute?

SAMUEL: Yeah, sure. What's on your mind?

ELI: When you asked mom to marry you. Did you have any doubts? I mean, were you absolutely certain you wanted to spend the rest of your life with her?

SAMUEL: What the hell prompted that question?

ELI: I'm thinking of asking Alison to marry me.

SAMUEL: *(Smiling.)* Is that right? Well, congratulations. She's a great girl and you'd be lucky to have her!

ELI: Yes, I know. She's a great girl.

SAMUEL: But? But what? You love her, don't you?

ELI: Yes, of course I do. Absolutely.

SAMUEL: So, what's the problem?

ELI: There's no problem! It's just for the rest of my life, and I want to make sure I'm making the right decision.

SAMUEL: Eli, that's not a decision you make with your mind, you make it with your heart.

ELI: Yes, I'm aware of that, but it's not that simple.

SAMUEL: The hell it isn't! You and your generation can't make a goddamn decision about anything because you overthink everything. You have a thousand options ranging from job opportunities to pizza toppings and it stops you in your tracks.

ELI: What is that supposed to mean?

SAMUEL: It means you got the best education money can buy. You graduated with two degrees and have spent the last six years dabbling with this career and that one, trying to decide what to *settle for.*

ELI: *(Defensive.)* I'm not trying to decide what to settle for! I'm exploring a few different paths before I commit the next forty years of my life to a career that I'll regret!

SAMUEL: *(A beat.)* Are you referring to my job? I don't regret running a metal supply business.

ELI: Dad, I've listened to you complain about your job my whole life.

SAMUEL: Yes, Eli. Every man complains about his job occasionally. Sometimes your employees screw up, or your cash flow runs short, or whatever the hell it is, but you deal with it each day and move on. My business has put food on our table for thirty years and bought us this house. It meant your mother didn't have to work, and it put you through Princeton, and I am damn proud of that!

ELI: Pop, I know you're proud of your business and you should be. I also know that your business gave you an ulcer. That you always wanted to do something else for a living and never did. You and Mom never traveled because you were sure the company would fall apart if you were gone for a week. That's not what I want for my life! I want a career that will not only put food on my table, but also bring me some joy and allow me to participate in other facets of my life.

SAMUEL: Then become a doctor! You're guaranteed a round of golf on Wednesdays.

(Eli regards his father, silently.)

SAMUEL: Eli, I want you to have a richer life than I've had, any father wants that for his son. On the other hand, I've always been a pragmatic man and you've been a dreamer since you were a kid. It's time you grow up and make a decision about your future and get on with it. Commit to it.

ELI: I'm going to!

SAMUEL: I'm not finished. And, as far as getting married? You asked me if I was certain about spending the rest of my life with your mother? Yes, I was. You ask yourself these simple questions: Do I love this woman? Does she love me? Do I want her to be the mother of my children? Will I be a better man because of her? If you can answer yes to those questions, then she's the woman you're supposed to spend your future with. *(He pauses.)* I have some regrets in my life, but never once has that included marrying your mother. She's the best thing that ever happened to me and I've spent my life trying to make her proud, trying to ensure that she never regretted saying yes to me.

ELI: *(A gentle smile.)* I don't think she's ever regretted it, Pop.

SAMUEL: Then I wish you and Alison the same luck we've had.

(Eli nods appreciatively, and Samuel walks across the room and hugs him.)

SAMUEL: A grandchild in the near future wouldn't be a bad thing either.

ELI: *(Glib.)* How did I know that was coming?

(Samuel shrugs, and walks back to his desk, smiling.)

Notes to Greg and Russell Scene

The major stumbling block between these two men is Russell's reluctance to publicly acknowledge their relationship. Greg doesn't doubt Russell's commitment, but resents being excluded from facets of his partner's life. Greg is very comfortable with his sexuality, whereas Russell is reluctant to reveal his preference, still concerned with social acceptance.

The totality of Greg's invective through the scene is ultimately explained by a single sentence, "I just wanted you to want me there." Russell's unwillingness to take Greg to his office party strikes at the core of Greg's insecurity and unleashes a tirade of anger and recrimination.

Usually their arguments don't escalate to this level because Russell generally refuses to engage in Greg's histrionics, a dynamic that creates ongoing conflict between them. On this occasion, Greg won't allow Russell to diffuse his anger and goads Russell into unleashing his own pent-up emotion.

It's important to allow the drama and the heightened emotion in the first two pages to be offset by the quietness and simplicity of the final page. In the heat of the moment, both said hurtful things they'll regret, but the caring and commitment continues.

GREG and RUSSELL

Two gay men battle about their relationship.
The door opens and Greg and Russell enter, in the midst of an argu-
ment. Russell is the older of the two, very rational and calm, in contrast
to Greg's emotional nature.

RUSSELL: Why do you have to make such a big production out of this?

GREG: Because it is a big production! I consider you not wanting to take
me to your Christmas party a flat out insult. There's no other way
to look at it!

RUSSELL: *(Measured.)* Of course there is. There's the rational way to look
at it. I don't want to take you not because I'm ashamed of you, but
because I don't feel it's appropriate at this point to share my private
life with my office, okay? What part of that do you not understand?

GREG: Don't talk to me like I'm an idiot. I hate when you do that.

RUSSELL: Oh stop it.

GREG: Russell, we've been living together for six months. I deserve to be
introduced to the people you work with. I deserve to be acknowl-
edged as the man you share a house with.

RUSSELL: This isn't about what *you* deserve. It's about what *I* deserve, which
is privacy! For Christ's sake, Greg, I've only worked at this firm for
five months and as far as I'm concerned, my personal life is no one's
business.

GREG: Your dirty little secret, is that it?

RUSSELL: Here we go again . . .

GREG: That's right! You live a life of hypocrisy and it sickens me. You're
no closer now than you were a year ago to admitting the truth about
who you are. You're a gay man, Russell! Accept it. Deal with it. Admit it!

RUSSELL: Unlike you, I don't feel the need to join the gay parade and shout
about my *pride!* I have no trouble admitting that I'm gay. I just don't
feel the need to flaunt it in front of every human being I meet. I
think discretion is a lesson you could stand to learn.

GREG: Oh, spare me! Every time I bring this up, you get defensive.

RUSSELL: I'm not being defensive. It's simply that we go about things in a different way and you need to respect that my way isn't wrong, just because it doesn't jive with yours.

GREG: Your way is hypocritical. What exactly should I respect about that?

RUSSELL: Give it a rest! You're beginning to sound more and more like my ex-wife. Whining and complaining that I'm not the man you wish I were.

GREG: Well, no mystery there. We've both lived with a man who wants to pretend he's straight! I actually pity her. At least in the dark, you sleep with me.

RUSSELL: Don't get ugly, Greg.

GREG: It's your truth. You wanna call it ugly, go ahead!

RUSSELL: That's enough. I've told you a hundred times . . .

GREG: You're the one that brought up your ex-wife, not me! You hid behind your marriage for ten years. I thought by the time I met you that you had come out! That those conflicts were over. Obviously, they're not.

RUSSELL: This conversation is tiresome. I have no conflict about what I am or who I choose to be with. I simply am discreet about who I share that information with. If you can't accept that, I'll pack up and leave. Is that what you want?

GREG: What I want is for you to be comfortable enough with us not to care who knows! Is that asking too much?

RUSSELL: It's asking more than I can do.

GREG: Then this has no future.

RUSSELL: Greg, we deal with the fact that you're extroverted, I'm not. I'm punctual, you're not. I earn money, you spend it. It's our differences that work.

GREG: No. Our differences, we accept. This difference, I can't! This is not negotiable.

RUSSELL: Fine. Then, let's call it a day. I can't turn myself inside out for you and I'm sick of trying.

GREG: What's that supposed to mean?

RUSSELL: It means that you want me to be ten years younger, ten pounds thinner, more flamboyant, more like you! None of that is going to happen. You want out of this relationship and this is the perfect excuse.

GREG: I can't believe what I'm hearing.

RUSSELL: It's the way I see it.

GREG: *(Anguished.)* I do not want out of this relationship, Russell! I just want to be more included in your life!

(They stare at each other for a moment, without speaking. Finally, Russell walks over to the table, picks up the party invitation, and hands it to Greg.)

RUSSELL: *(Contrite.)* Come with me to the party.

GREG: *(Reading the invitation.)* . . . Black tie, boring lawyers, terrible food and watered-down drinks. I'll pass.

RUSSELL: Now you don't want to go?

GREG: *(Sincere.)* I never wanted to go. I just wanted you to want me there.

(Russell shakes his head, the corners of his mouth turning up.)

RUSSELL: You're gonna make me crazy.

GREG: *(Smiles.)* I'm worth it.

Notes to Oliver and Bill Scene

This scene has a quiet sadness to it. These two brothers have not seen each other in several years and have come together for the funeral of their father. Bill feels the gravity of his father's death much more than Oliver, and reveals his monumental sense of loss to his brother.

Oliver is the older brother and a successful, independent man. He left home when he was nineteen and never looked back. His involvement in his career has precluded him from sharing the lives of his family, both his parents and brother as well as his own wife and children. The death of his father has made him more conscious of his neglect and the need to reconnect with his family.

Bill is a gentle soul, kind, thoughtful and idealistic. He never outgrew his youthful dependence on his father and it has contributed to his weakness. In the aftermath of his father's death, he is totally bereft. He is painfully aware of his own shortcomings, and his lack of self-confidence contributes to his vulnerability.

Throughout this scene, the difference in Bill and Oliver's emotions is apparent. Oliver reflects on his father with fondness but not with grief. Bill's sadness and despair is very close to the surface, and he struggles to fight back his tears until he talks about missing his father and the impact he had on his life. For the first time, Oliver truly realizes the extent of his brother's pain and attempts to comfort him by offering words of support and insight into his own failings.

OLIVER and BILL

*Two middle-age brothers at very different places in their lives talk at the
service following the funeral of their father.*
*Bill stands alone in a corner, lost in thought. His older brother, Oliver,
approaches and hugs him.*

OLIVER: How are you holding up?

BILL: All right, I guess. How about you?

OLIVER: The same. It's been nice seeing some of Dad's old friends, though.
Even under the circumstances.

BILL: It's probably been ten years since you've seen some of these people.

OLIVER: At least. I can't believe how old they look. I know they're about
the same age as Dad was, but he never looked old to me.

BILL: Well, he took good care of himself. You know, for an eighty-year-
old guy, he was pretty agile. He still took his daily swim, puttered
around the garage, pretty girls still turned his head . . .

OLIVER: You're kiddin' me.

BILL: No. He never did it when Mom was around, but when I'd take him
out to lunch, I'd catch him looking for a minute and then he'd chuckle
to himself, you know, the way he did that.

OLIVER: I loved that quality of his. He'd say, "Sometimes I just think funny
thoughts!"

BILL: *(Smiling sadly.)* I think he had a good life. He didn't ask for much
and was content with what he had. I suppose there's a lesson to be
learned there.

OLIVER: I envy you the time you had with him in the last few years. I
kept meaning to get down here more often, but something always
came up. I should have just made the time, there's no excuse for it.
I knew he wasn't going to be around forever.

BILL: He knew you worked hard, Oliver. You probably should visit Mom
more often though. This isn't going to be easy for her.

OLIVER: I know. Lauren already asked her if she wanted to come back to
New Haven with us for a few weeks. I hope we can talk her into it.

BILL: I do too. It'll be tough for her being alone in this house. I wanted her to move in with us for awhile, but I know she'll never agree to it.

OLIVER: She and Mandy still don't get along?

BILL: *(Shaking his head.)* What can I say? My wife's a bitch and she's getting worse every year.

OLIVER: I don't know why you stay with her. Why do you?

BILL: Good question. I moved out last year, did you know that?

OLIVER: No. You never mentioned it. Dad didn't either.

BILL: He didn't know. I moved into a hotel for a few weeks. I missed the boys so much I was miserable. Mandy promised she'd change, so I came back. She was great for about a month, and then she started bitching again and we were back where we started.

OLIVER: You deserve better, you know that.

BILL: I guess.

OLIVER: Look, why don't you come to New Haven as well? It can't be good for your kids with all the tension in your house. Bring the boys and come stay with us for a week. We have plenty of room.

BILL: Thanks, I'll think about it. The last few days I've been on autopilot. You know, at the hospital, and making the funeral arrangements and all that. It's hard to take it all in. *(His eyes fill up with tears.)* I'm really going to miss him.

OLIVER: *(Gently.)* I know.

BILL: No you don't! You moved away years ago and made your own life. I never got more than ten blocks away. Do you realize that? I live ten blocks away from the house we grew up in. I went into business with Dad. Even after he retired, I still talked to him every day and asked for advice. For Christ's sake, I'm forty years old and I still depended on my father for guidance! No wonder I never had the courage to leave my wife. How are my boys ever going to have the respect for me that I had for him?

(Bill averts his eyes and quickly wipes away his tears. Oliver looks at his brother with compassion and sadness.)

OLIVER: Billy, you're a good man. You're a good father and a kind human being. Your boys have plenty to look up to. There's no shame in the choices you've made.

(Oliver pats Bill on the shoulder.)

OLIVER: Dad always told me I was so busy chasing my dreams that I missed out on life. He was right. I've spent years thinking I had to work harder, earn more money, and my wife and daughters have paid the price for it. We have a beautiful big house and I'm rarely in it.

BILL: Whatever road you choose, I guess it's hard to get it right. You know, when we were kids, I figured by the time we got to be this age we'd have all the answers, like Dad did.

OLIVER: Dad didn't have all the answers, Bill.

BILL: Yeah, but I thought he did. That's what mattered to me.

Notes to Gene and Ricky Scene

Gene Barrett is a seasoned college football coach. He's a good coach: knowledgeable, direct, insightful and compassionate. He feels paternal toward his team and knows enough about the psychology of athletes to know when to encourage them and when to challenge them.

Ricky Rawlins is a gifted athlete, told since he was a kid that football was his destiny. He was young when his mother died, and his father raised him alone, investing all his dreams into his son. He carries the weight of his father's sacrifices.

Ricky is deeply conflicted about realizing his own ambitions and satisfying his father's wishes. When he discusses his father in the scene, he finally allows himself to express both the resentment and sadness he's kept bottled up for years.

When the scene opens, both Gene and the audience believe that Ricky is defying the advice of his coach because he's hellbent on playing football and believes himself impervious to serious injury. Suddenly, Gene realizes that Ricky's determination is not the voice of ego but the voice of desperation. He's got to make it far enough to satisfy his father but not far enough to endure a career he doesn't want.

There is a lot of shading to Ricky's character. He feels indebted to his father but also embittered that he wasn't allowed to pursue his own goals. This is probably the first time Rick has admitted those feelings to anyone other than himself. They are not spoken with anger but with guilt and conflict.

Gene's character recognizes that this is not an easy admission for Rick and knows that by encouraging him to finally break free of his father's influence, he'll take some responsibility for the conflict that will ensue. He is kind, but challenges Ricky to behave like an adult and take control of his own life.

GENE and RICKY

A college football coach confronts a player about his future.
Ricky Rawlins, a senior running-back, sits on a chair with his leg ele-
vated, facing his coach, Gene Barrett.

GENE: Ricky, I'm sending you over to get an MRI. We need to know
whether you've sprained the ligament again or torn it altogether.

RICKY: Coach, I'm telling ya, I didn't tear it. I'll ice it and wear the brace,
and in two weeks, I'll be fine.

GENE: Listen up. If you've torn both the collateral ligament and the cru-
ciate ligament, you need surgery. End of conversation.

RICKY: No way! I go in for surgery, and it takes six months to get back
in shape.

GENE: And if you don't have surgery, you could end up hobbling around
for the rest of your life.

RICKY: The East-West game is next month! If I don't play in that game,
my future goes down the drain.

GENE: Bullshit. You're the best running back in the history of this school.
You run the 40 in 4.4 — You ran 1700 yards this year. The agents
know about you already and you've got a good shot at being drafted.

RICKY: Being drafted isn't enough! I've gotta be in the top ten! This is Chico
State not Florida State These guys need to see me compete against
the best, and the only way that's gonna happen is if I play in the All-
Star game.

GENE: Even if your ligament's sprained and not torn, you still won't be
able to run full out. You may play, but you won't play up to capacity.

RICKY: The hell I won't.

GENE: You're dreamin' Rick. I've coached for eighteen years, I've seen these
injuries before, and you're going to do permanent damage to yourself.

RICKY: Why are you trying so hard to stop me? If I get drafted to the Raiders
or the Broncos, it'll sure up your status as a coach.

GENE: Yep. But not enough for me to risk your future.

RICKY: It's my future, not yours. I'll take my chances.

(Gene stares at Ricky, long and hard, then suddenly responds.)

GENE: You don't want to play pro ball, do you?

RICKY: What?

GENE: You don't. This is all bullshit. You know your knees won't hold up. You've just got to prove to your father that you were good enough for the pro's to want you.

RICKY: You're outta your mind.

(Gene walks over to Ricky and leans into his face.)

GENE: I don't think so. You're too smart to be this stupid. You've got legs that could carry you to the Super Bowl. If you really wanted a future in football, you'd do everything you could to protect yourself. You wouldn't risk cutting short your career!

(Ricky looks away. Gene nods, knowing he's hit a nerve.)

GENE: I'll be damned.

(Ricky takes a long pause before responding.)

RICKY: My dad's whole life is my football career. He's been at every game I've ever played, got every trophy I've ever won on the mantle. If I get a four-million-dollar contract, he can retire for life. How do I take that away from him?

GENE: It's your life, Rick, not his.

RICKY: Yeah. You tell him that.

GENE: I'll tell *you* something: To make a career out of football, you've gotta be more than just a gifted athlete. Your hearts gotta be in the game. Yours never has been.

RICKY: Well, maybe it woulda been, if he hadn't shoved it down my throat since Pop Warner!

GENE: What is it you want to do, Ricky?

RICKY: I want to be a doctor.

(Gene's mouth falls open, totally stunned.)

RICKY: What? You don't think I could? I get good grades.

GENE: Yeah, you do. Surprisingly good grades for a ballplayer.

RICKY: That's right. My mom died of cancer when I was thirteen. My aunt died last year. As far as I can tell, no one's doin' shit to make this disease go away. I want to try.

GENE: Then do it. Curing cancer beats the hell out of going to the Super Bowl.

RICKY: Yeah. And like you said, I probably wouldn't hobble around for the rest of my life.

GENE: Look, let's get you an MRI. I'll bet even money you need surgery, and that takes the all-star game off the table.

RICKY: This is gonna kill my dad.

GENE: He'll live with it, Rick. You want me to talk to him?

RICKY: No! It's not your place. It's mine.

GENE: Then tell him the truth. I'd think having your kid become a doctor would be more than enough for him.

RICKY: *(Wistful.)* You'd think so, wouldn't you?

The Author

Dorian Dunas attended USC film school and began work in the business as a scriptreader for Director Richard Donner.

She worked for years in development and film production, then began work in casting. Her first job as a casting assistant was *Pretty in Pink*.

Through the years she has worked on eleven features, five television series, six pilots, and two plays. In addition to her work as a casting director, she began writing. The first comedy script she co-wrote was optioned by Paramount Pictures.

She continues to cast both feature films and television and is writing a new script.